YOUR KNOWLEDGE H

Bibliographic information published by the German National Library:

The German National Library lists this publication in the National Bibliography; detailed bibliographic data are available on the Internet at http://dnb.dnb.de .

Imprint:

Copyright © 2019 GRIN Verlag
Print and binding: Books on Demand GmbH, Norderstedt Germany
ISBN: 9783346214416

This book at GRIN:

https://www.grin.com/document/901784

Kristina Kraljevic

The change from amortised costs to fair value regarding the International Financial Reporting Standards 9

GRIN Verlag

GRIN - Your knowledge has value

Since its foundation in 1998, GRIN has specialized in publishing academic texts by students, college teachers and other academics as e-book and printed book. The website www.grin.com is an ideal platform for presenting term papers, final papers, scientific essays, dissertations and specialist books.

Visit us on the internet:

http://www.grin.com/

http://www.facebook.com/grincom

http://www.twitter.com/grin_com

The change from amortised costs to fair value regarding the International Financial Reporting Standards 9

Master thesis

Submitted by: **Kristina Kraljević, BA**

at **Fachhochschul-Masterstudiengang
(European Finance and Risk
Management)**

Wiener Neustadt, 25 August 2019

Kurzzusammenfassung

Die folgende Arbeit beschäftigt sich mit den International Financial Reporting Standards 9 und deren Änderungen, welche seit 1. Januar 2018 umzusetzen sind. Der Fokus liegt auf den Regelungen von IFRS 9 für finanzielle Verbindlichkeiten, wobei der Großteil der Regelungen den International Accounting Standards 39 entspricht. Eine wesentliche Änderung durch IFRS 9 ist die Erfolgserfassung von finanziellen Verbindlichkeiten bei der Ausübung der Fair-Value-Option. Demzufolge ist die Erfassung von Änderungen, die auf die eigene Bonität zurückzuführen sind, im sonstigen Ergebnis auszuweisen.

Schlagworte

IFRS 9, IAS 39, Marktwert, fortgeführte Anschaffungskosten, Fair-Value-Option, sonstige Ergebnis

Abstract

This paper examines the adaption of the International Financial Reporting Standards 9, effective as of 1 January 2018. The introduction outlines the reasons for the amendments and the objectives of IFRS 9 which are divided into three phases. The focus of this paper is the effect of IFRS 9 on financial liabilities. While the International Accounting Standards 39 for financial liabilities are still accurate, IFRS 9 lead to a change in the fair value option. As a result, changes in the fair value which are caused by the own credit risk are booked into the other comprehensive income.

Keywords

IFRS 9, IAS 39, fair value, amortised cost, fair value option, other comprehensive income

Table of contents

List of abbreviations

Abbreviation	Meaning / Explanation
AC	Amortised cost(s)
AFS	Available for sale
AKt_0	Acquisition cost at t_0
ALM	Asset Liability Management
BCBS	Basel Committee on Banking Supervision
BIS	Bank for International Settlements
CFt_i	Cash flows including interest and capital payment
CRD	Capital Requirements Directive
CRR	Capital Requirements Regulation
EAD	Exposure at default
ECB	European Central Bank
ECL	Expected credit loss model
Erste Group AG	Erste Group Bank Aktiengesellschaft
EURIBOR	Euro Interbank Offered Rate
FASB	Financial Accounting Standards Board
FIFO	First in – First out
FINREP	Financial Reporting Standards
FV	Fair value
FVO	Fair value option
FVOCI	Fair value through other comprehensive income
FVTPL	Fair value through profit or loss
HTM	Held to maturity
IAS	International Accounting Standards
IASB	International Accounting Standards Board
IASC	International Accounting Standards Committee
ICAAP	Internal Capital Adequacy Assessment Process
IFRIC	International Financial Reporting Interpretations Committee
IFRS	International Financial Reporting Standards
ISMA	International Securities Market Association
L&R	Loans and receivables

LGD	Loss given default
n	Maturity/Interest rate adjustment date
NII	Net Interest Income
OCI	Other comprehensive income
OTC	Over the counter
P & L	Profit-and-loss account
PD	Probability of default
RBI AG	Raiffeisen Bank International Aktiengesellschaft
r_{eff}	Effective interest rate
SIC	Standard Interpretations Committee
SIIs	Systemically important institutions
SIs	Significant institutions
SPPI	Solely Payments of Principal and Interest
SREP	Supervisory Review and Evaluation Process
SSM	Single Supervisory Mechanism
t_0	Valuation date
t_i	Time of the CFt_i payment
US-GAAP	United States Generally Accepted Accounting Principles

1 Introduction

The introduction of this master thesis outlines the research interest and research question. Furthermore, the objective of the examination, the relevance and the level of research regarding the topic of IFRS 9 is described.

1.1 Research interest & Research question

Apart from applying the International Accounting Standards (IAS) 39, the execution of practical implementation of the International Financial Reporting Standards (IFRS) 9 must be finalised as of January 1st of 2018. According to the press release of the International Accounting Standards Board (IASB) in November 2009, the main objectives of IFRS 9 were divided into three phases. The first phase includes alterations regarding the classification and measurement. In contrast, phase two deals with amortised cost and impairment, whereas the third phase focuses on hedge accounting (International Accounting Standards Board 2009, 1).

This paper aims to give an overview on the relevant changes regarding IFRS 9. However, the main focus is set at the liabilities side, the classification and the measurement of financial liabilities. Although the IASB intended to create a model in order to classify financial instruments of both the asset and the liabilities side, it had to prioritise the asset side owing to the financial crisis and the demand for new regulations in 2009. Therefore, the research context considers the adjustment of the fair value option (FVO) treatment. Due to the new regulation, changes in the own credit spread or rather the creditworthiness need to be captured under the position "other comprehensive income" (OCI), which affects the net income. Unless the financial liability is designated as FVO, the subsequent measurement of the liability follows amortised cost (Deloitte & Touche GmbH Wirtschaftsprüfungsgesellschaft 2011, 35f.).

However, choosing the FVO implies that once the change in the credit spread has been recorded under the OCI, the amount is not reclassified into the profit-and-loss account (P & L). In contrast to that, a reclassification is permitted within equity e.g. a financial liability designated at FVO that is derecognised (Deloitte & Touche GmbH Wirtschaftsprüfungsgesellschaft 2014, 15f.).

The reason for the new regulation is based on IAS 39 and the measurement of liabilities in regard to the credit spread. Although, the creditworthiness deteriorated during the financial crisis, financial institutions had to realise the increasing credit spread in the P & L as an earning and a decreasing fair value (FV) of the liability. This mixed-model approach is a reason for the volatility in P & L's and has been revised in the course of the IFRS 9 (Becker and Wiechens 2008, 625f.; Lane and Kennedy 2015).

With the mandatory implementation of the new set of regulations 2018 onwards, the central question is as follows:

"What is the impact of IFRS 9 regarding liabilities?"

1.2 Objective of the examination

Due to the fact that IFRS 9 has been valid since the beginning of 2018, the aim of this research is to define the consequences of moving from amortised cost (AC) to FV measurement. Consequently, the valuation principles for liabilities based on IFRS 9 are described and three banking products on the liability side (deposits from customers, deposits from banks and own issuances) are evaluated. Moreover, a comparison of these banking products in terms of conditions and measurement before and after the introduction of IFRS 9 shall provide examples to determine whether applying the FVO is necessary. Therefore, the consolidated financial statements of Raiffeisen Bank International Aktiengesellschaft (RBI AG) and Erste Group Bank Aktiengesellschaft (Erste Group AG) in 2017, 2018 and the interim report of the first quarter of 2019 are examined.

1.3 Relevance

The most relevant reason for the composition and introduction of the IFRS 9 is attributable to the financial crisis. Several global and domestic systemically important banks, amongst other Goldman Sachs, faced difficulties during the economic downturn. According to a "The New York Times" article published by Jenny Anderson and Landon Thomas Jr. in November 2007, Goldman Sachs was the only bank being able to forecast mortgage risk. However, Goldman Sachs continued selling risky mortgage securities to its investors in order to reduce speculative assets in their portfolio. Further, the bank decided to buy an insurance for the case of future losses. While Goldman Sachs had the highest write-downs amounting to USD 1.5 billion, it still managed to achieve a profit of USD 2.85 billion in the third quarter by selling risky mortgage securities to other banks such as Merrill Lynch, Citigroup and Morgan Stanley (Anderson and Thomas Jr. 2007).

In 2008, Ben Whitedec's article in "The New York Times" dealt with Goldman Sachs and its quarterly loss of USD 2.1 billion. While it was able to manage the mortgage risk in 2007, Goldman Sachs did not consider the declining tendency in the global equity markets. As a result, the trading and investment business lost USD 4.36 billion and Goldman Sachs' long-term senior debt ratings were downgraded from Aa3 to A1 by Moody's, which led to a drastical shortening of compensations, expenses and benefits (Whitedec 2008).

Nevertheless, IFRS provides a framework for accounting and considers two characteristics, relevance and reliability and their interaction. On the one hand, an accounting department is allocated the task to deliver relevant information, which is from an investor's point of view information concerning the near future. On the other hand, it prescribes the necessity for accounting to publish reliable information. As no precise prediction exists for the future, a distinction must exist between the use of fair value and historical costs (Blecher 2018).

Moreover, transparency and comparability of data is important for a sound banking supervision in accordance with the regulations, as IFRS is only valid for stock-listed banks in the European Union (Boissieu 2017, 86). In addition, the new regulations of IFRS also intend to simplify the comparison between European reporting standards and the United States Generally Accepted Accounting Principles (US-GAAP) (Kobialka 2017, 226). Although this paper is relevant for capital market oriented companies, it also addresses potential users such as shareholders, lenders, customers, suppliers and other stakeholders interested in the topic of IFRS 9 (Müller and Saile 2018, 17).

1.4 Current state of research

The advantages and disadvantages of the introduction of IFRS 9 are handled in various books and publications. A key reason for the mandatory applicability of IFRS 9 was the complex and detailed rules of IAS 39 regarding financial assets. In addition, the FV valuation is referred to as the result for the financial crisis. Therefore, IFRS 9 shall facilitate accounting and improve the issue of FV determination and cost accounting (Kobialka 2017, 225f.).

In an article written by Christian Blecher, the topic of FV and cost accounting is discussed. The author claims to have observed that a FV might be manipulated whereas cost accounting usually is not affected. In such cases it is difficult to evaluate whether the future turns out as favourably as forecasted (Blecher 2018).

On grounds of the previously mentioned, IFRS 9 aim to simplify accounting rules and enable comparison between others. In addition, subsequent measurement has also been facilitated as IAS 39 allowed for various valuation procedures and an undefined number of input parameters, while IFRS 9 have specified formulae, enabling verifiability (Kirsten 2016, 195f.).

However, the previously conducted research shows different outcomes regarding the FV treatment. According to an essay written by Klaus Becker and Gero Wiechens, financial institutions were able to take advantage of the FVO due to increasing credit spreads in 2017. Nevertheless, there is still a vast variety of spreads, e.g. funding spread or credit default swap spread, which leaves room for flexibility and the lack of comparability. An additional matter discussed in the essay is the interaction between an increasing credit spread and a decreasing FV which does not have an effect on the asset side but on the equity (Becker and Wiechens 2008, 627ff.).

Another research conducted by Wei Wu, Nicole Thibodeau and Robert Couch aimed to evaluate if the usage of the FVO favoured adverse selection during the financial crisis. The results showed that mainly companies exposed to financial problems were opting for the FV approach in order to achieve income despite rising credit spreads (Wu, Thibodeau and Couch 2016, 474).

In contrast to that, the descriptive study from Felix Schneider and Duc Hung Tran provided a completely opposite result. The study focuses on European banks from 2006 to 2010 and indicates that the FVO does not come along with high credit spreads but rather shows lower bid-ask spreads compared to banks not using the FVO. Even though the FVO does not influence the level of transparency, it is also mentioned that the paper is only descriptive and the identification of effects solely regarding the FVO are difficult (Schneider and Tran 2015, 1007f.).

Furthermore, a study of Brian Bratten, Monika Causholli and Urooj Khan discusses the usage of the FV and the relevance of the OCI. The findings indicate that the OCI based on the FV supports the estimation of earnings for the time horizon of one to two years. Moreover, the FV approach delivers information in order to meet reporting standards (Bratten, Causholli and Khan 2016, 310).

However, Dominic Detzen's paper criticises the OCI as the interpretation relies on the utilisation of standard setters. In addition, the OCI is seen as a position for volatility and lacks definition and guidance which might favour going against the regulations (Detzen 2016, 777f.).

2 Description of the methodical approach

The method design includes three points. To begin with, the consolidated financial statements of 2017, 2018 and the interim report for the first quarter of 2019 from RBI AG and Erste Group AG are analysed and compared to each other regarding the classification and measurement of liabilities. In addition to that, the measurement and the treatment of the three banking products before and after the introduction of the new regulations are compared to the results of RBI AG and Erste Group AG. This indicates that a concrete example is evaluated from a theoretical point of view and afterwards compared to the results from the annual statements of banks. Therefore, following contents of the consolidated financial statements are illustrated:

- statement of comprehensive income
- statement of financial position
- statement of financial position according to the measurement categories
- composition of each liability
- breakdown of maturities

As IFRS 9 is mandatory since 2018, it is reasonable to assume that publications of consolidated financial statements meet the requirements of IFRS 9.

3 International Financial Reporting Standards 9

As companies tend to increase international presence through opening subsidiaries abroad, the demand to refinance the business occurs throughout capital markets. In order to facilitate globalisation, financial statements need to be transparent and comparable, resulting in time and cost reduction. Furthermore, the banking sector benefits from standard guidelines as it obtains funds but also lends loans to private customers and businesses. However, it is important to point out that financial accounting depends on national, international and European standards. The IFRS and the accounting method, which is defined by the European Union in 2005, is obligatory for capital market oriented companies (PricewaterhouseCoopers Aktiengesellschaft Wirtschafts-prüfungsgesellschaft 2017a, 177f. and 181).

3.1 Principles of the International Financial Reporting Standards Framework

In general, the system of IFRS is split into the framework, the standards including IFRS and IAS, the interpretation of the International Financial Reporting Interpretations Committee (IFRIC) and the Standard Interpretations Committee (SIC). This chapter focuses on the framework and reflects the theoretical input of the financial accounting standards (PricewaterhouseCoopers Aktiengesellschaft Wirtschaftsprüfungsgesellschaft 2017a, 295 and 297).

The principles of the IFRS framework are described in the IAS 1 and focuses on the presentation of financial statements. This chapter highlights the most relevant principles such as:

- the fair presentation and compliance with IFRS,
- the going concern principle,
- the accrual basis of accounting,
- the materiality and the aggregation,
- the offsetting,
- the frequency of reporting and
- the comparative information (Müller and Saile 2018, 14).

First of all, IAS 1.15-24 aims for a fair presentation and compliance with IFRS, which is also considered as true-and-fair-view-principle. This fair presentation is relevant for the financial position, financial performance and cash flows. However, this generally described standard further requires to apply the accounting policies, changes in accounting, estimates and errors set in the IFRS 8 (Müller and Saile 2018, 14).

Secondly, the framework sets in IAS 1.25-26 the going concern principle leading managers to make assumptions about the future development of the business at least for the next twelve months starting from the latest reporting period. However, if a company intends to dissolve its business the principle is ineffective (Müller and Saile 2018, 19).

Furthermore, the accrual basis of accounting in IAS 1.27-28 is of relevance for assets, liabilities, equity and income and expenses. Therefore, this principle sets the definitions and requirements for the categorisation (Müller and Saile 2018, 20). In addition, materiality and aggregation considers relevant information for accounting and the merge of similar items based on the materiality. Nevertheless, this principle shown in IAS 1.29-31 is not allowing for covering up unfavourable conditions in order to manipulate financial statements (Müller and Saile 2018, 15f.).

Regarding the items, IAS 1.32-35 prescribe that assets cannot net liabilities out which as well applies to income and expenses. While certain exceptions for offsetting made by IFRS might exist, materiality plays an important role insofar as it allows for aggregation of similar items, for instance gains and losses resulting from currency conversion (Müller and Saile 2018, 23).

The framework requests a company to publish financial statements at least yearly according to IAS 1.36-37 (Müller and Saile 2018, 23). Further, IAS 1.38-44 focus on comparative information. In this case, it requires to include figures and other relevant information of the previous reporting period into the financial statement. Whereas these are the minimum comparative information, further details are provided for additional comparative information as well as for change in accounting policy, retrospective restatement or reclassification (Institut der Wirtschaftsprüfer 2018, 231).

Finally, IAS 1.45-46 are also of relevance with regards to the comparative information concerning the presentation of financial statements. As a result, the presentation of financial statements shall be consistent and thereby facilitate the comparability of previous reporting periods (Müller and Saile 2018, 22).

3.2 Main amendments

With the financial crisis the IASB faced the demand for a review of the existing standards, especially IAS 39 regarding the recognition and measurement of financial instruments. The process started with the "IAS 39 Replacement Project" in November 2008 with the main focus at enabling comparability of financial statements under IFRS and reduce complexity for the accounting of financial instruments (Sagerschnig 2016, 3).

However, the initial version of IAS 39 which is known as interim standard, was published in 1999 by the International Accounting Standards Committee (IASC). Even before the financial crisis, IAS 39 was considered as a complex issue and the IASB and the Financial Accounting Standards Board (FASB) released a "Memorandum of Understanding" which aimed at establishing generally valid accounting standards for the capital markets. As a result, the consultation paper "Reducing Complexity in Reporting Financial Instruments" was rolled out by the IASB and FASB in March 2008 (Deloitte & Touche GmbH Wirtschaftsprüfungsgesellschaft 2011, 3f.).

In addition to the comparability and reduction of complexity, a further aim of IFRS 9 is to follow a principle-based model instead of a rule-based model for classifying financial instruments. Furthermore, the business model and the contractual cash flows are considered. Regarding the changes for impairments, expected losses are included allowing to improve the quality of risk management. Finally, inconsistencies between risk management and hedge accounting are removed (Sagerschnig 2016, 3).

Due to the length and the various contents of the project, the IASB decided to split the topics in the following three phases: classification and measurement, amortised cost and impairment and hedge accounting (Deloitte & Touche GmbH Wirtschaftsprüfungsgesellschaft 2014, 2).

3.2.1 Phase I – Classification and Measurement

Phase one discusses the classification and measurement of financial assets and liabilities. To begin with, the initial recognition is described in IFRS 9.3.1.1 and states that a financial asset or liability is solely recorded if a contracting party of the financial instrument exists. In addition, the paragraph refers to the standards in IFRS which set the classification and measurement of financial assets and liabilities (Sagerschnig 2016, 4).

In regard to financial assets, two main adjustments are made: the establishment of the business model and the contractual cash flow. To begin with, the business model is assessed on an aggregated level. As a result, the aim of a group of financial assets is of relevance instead of considering the objective of a single financial asset. Furthermore, it is required to assess the business model itself which can be deemed as a discretionary decision as any relevant fact or circumstance needs to be considered e.g. evaluating the efficiency of business model or risks affecting the business model and financial instruments. In addition, the contractual cash flows are introduced for the classification of financial instruments. Within the business model, three approaches for the contractual cash flows are distinguished: amounts allocated to the revenue resulting from contractual cash flows of financial assets held, selling financial assets to achieve contractual cash flows and a combination of the first and second approach (Deloitte & Touche GmbH Wirtschafts-prüfungsgesellschaft 2014, 6).

Consequently, a financial instrument is categorised in line with the business model and the contractual cash flow. While IAS 39 offered four classification categories, IFRS 9.4.1.1 allow only for two or alternatively for three classification categories depending on the interpretation. However, this paper

8

considers three classification categories for financial assets which are AC, fair value through other comprehensive income (FVOCI) and fair value through profit and loss (FVTPL) (Deloitte & Touche GmbH Wirtschaftsprüfungs-gesellschaft 2011, 9). Consequently, IAS 39.45 and its classification categories fair value through profit or loss, held to maturity (HTM), loans and receivables (L&R) as well as available for sale (AFS) are adapted or called off (Müller and Saile 2018, 145).

With regard to the measurement of financial assets, IFRS 9.4.1.2 set the measurement at AC for financial assets based on two conditions. First of all, the business model aims to achieve contractual cash flows by holding assets and secondly, the contractual term is of relevance for the dates when payments of the principal and interest are paid on the principal amount outstanding. Due to the definition, equity instruments and resulting dividend payments are excluded from this measurement. Furthermore, the measurement at AC requests that both the business model and the contractual cash flow criteria are met. In case a criterion is not met according to the standard, the measurement is at FVTPL in line with IFRS 9.4.1.4 (Deloitte & Touche GmbH Wirtschaftsprüfungs-gesellschaft 2011, 10).

Apart from that, if the business model aims to achieve revenues from the contractual cash flows of assets held and intends to sell assets, the financial asset is measured at FVOCI. The prerequisite, however, is that the contractual term of the dates when payments of the principal and interest are paid on the principal amount outstanding is fulfilled. This method is equivalent to the contractual cash flow of financial assets measured at AC (Deloitte & Touche GmbH Wirtschaftsprüfungsgesellschaft 2014, 8).

With reference to the business model, financial assets that are initially held for the purpose of generating contractual cash flows may be sold occasionally. This does not require the adaption of the business model but rather depends on the available information considered for the initial categorisation. Should such sales be regularly conducted, resulting in a considerable amount and lacking an appropriate explanation for frequent execution, a reconsideration of the business model is advisable (Deloitte & Touche GmbH Wirtschaftsprüfungs-gesellschaft 2014, 6f.).

In comparison to that, a business model that intends to hold and sell financial assets in order to receive contractual cash flows is not demanded to review previously conducted sales. The reason for defining such a business model comply with guidelines dealing with liquidity or interest income (Deloitte & Touche GmbH Wirtschaftsprüfungsgesellschaft 2014, 8f.).

With regard to the business model, there is another approach to collect, focusing on financial instruments intended for dealing e.g. holding a financial asset and selling it after a time where the possibility exists to achieve profit. Most likely these transactions are settled on a short-term basis but also a derivative can be used. Consequently, financial assets or liabilities are measured at FVTPL (Deloitte & Touche GmbH Wirtschaftsprüfungsgesellschaft 2014, 8).

Additionally, the contractual cash flow condition and its specifications impact the measurement of a financial asset. As described, the contractual terms define a date at which payments of the principal and interest are paid on the principal amount outstanding. This definition is valid for cash flows generated from basic lending arrangements. The two relevant components for the contractual cash flow are the notional amount and interest. The notional amount is measured for initial recognition at FV. However, a redemption which leads to a decrease in the notional amount is not influencing the contractual cash flow condition. Considering the interest, it solely compensates for the time value of the money, the default risk which occurs from the principal amount outstanding and the costs resulting from basic lending arrangements e.g. administration costs or margins (Deloitte & Touche GmbH Wirtschaftsprüfungsgesellschaft 2014, 9f.).

Nevertheless, there are a few features to consider in order to assure that the contractual cash flow condition is fulfilled. In regard to the time value of the money, the interest rate might have an effect if interest is set for a year but the fixing is carried out monthly. Deciding on the significance and a possible modification of the time value of the money is conducted by a qualitative or respectively quantitative analysis. Assuming that the difference between the actual and the unmodified cash flows for the reporting period and the remaining time is considerable, the measurement follows neither AC nor FVOCI but FVTPL (Deloitte & Touche GmbH Wirtschaftsprüfungsgesellschaft 2014, 10).

In addition to the time value of the money, the amount and the date of the payments might change. Therefore, the contractual cash flow must be reviewed unless it solely includes payments of the principal and interest paid on the principal amount outstanding. Assuming a premature resignation exists, the contractual cash flow is valid if the FV of the right of cancellation is insignificant at the point of taking the asset. Therefore, a prematurity compensation payment is acceptable (Deloitte & Touche GmbH Wirtschaftsprüfungsgesellschaft 2014, 11).

In terms of significance, the contractual cash flow is also fulfilled considering contractual terms which are characterised as "de minimis" and "not genuine". "De minimis" result in a small effect, whereas "not genuine" illustrates that the contractual term is not "de minimis" but the probability of occurrence is very unlikely (Deloitte & Touche GmbH Wirtschaftsprüfungsgesellschaft 2014, 11).

Another aspect to consider is the contractually linked instrument. While the business model follows IFRS 9, the contractual cash flow includes further criteria which have to be fulfilled in terms of the reallocation of credit risk. In case the conditions are met, the financial instrument is measured at AC; otherwise at FV affecting the P & L (Deloitte & Touche GmbH Wirtschaftsprüfungsgesellschaft 2011, 20).

Nevertheless, even if the business model and contractual cash flow are set at AC, it is still possible to switch to FV. This is only allowed under the condition of an accounting mismatch, or with other words, that financial assets might be measured at AC while financial liabilities are measured at FV. However, the switch to the FVO is solely permitted at initial recognition and is non-reversible (Deloitte & Touche GmbH Wirtschaftsprüfungsgesellschaft 2011, 25f.).

Besides the FVO, the FVOCI is allowed to be exercised for equity instruments since the contractual cash flow condition is not met. Unless the option is exercised, the measurement is at FV. As a result, changes in the FV are recorded in the OCI instead of the P & L. Nevertheless, an equity instrument is permitted to be designated as FVOCI if no trading purpose exists (Deloitte & Touche GmbH Wirtschaftsprüfungsgesellschaft 2014, 13).

The switch from FV to FVOCI is conform with the requirements of the FVO. In this case, the FVOCI is only allowed at the initial recognition and this option right cannot be reversed. However, dividends must be recorded in the P & L (Deloitte & Touche GmbH Wirtschaftsprüfungsgesellschaft 2011, 31).

In regard to embedded derivatives, IFRS 9 do not demand for a separation of the derivative from the host contract if the financial asset is connected to the contract (Deloitte & Touche GmbH Wirtschaftsprüfungsgesellschaft 2011, 34). Finally, if the business model changes, the financial asset must be reclassified. The reclassification is conducted prospectively and thereby leads to a new business model for the reporting period on the date of the reclassification (Deloitte & Touche GmbH Wirtschaftsprüfungsgesellschaft 2014, 14).

Besides the classification and measurement of financial assets, the focus is set on financial liabilities which are also affected by the alterations within phase one. While the IASB initially aimed to develop a symmetrical model for the classification of financial assets and liabilities, the priority has been redirected on financial assets owing to the financial crisis in 2008. Nevertheless, the issue of classifying financial liabilities started in 2010 (Deloitte & Touche GmbH Wirtschaftsprüfungsgesellschaft 2011, 35).

In comparison to financial assets, the amount of changes for financial liabilities is less significant and most parts of IAS 39 are still valid in IFRS 9. The classification and measurement is either at AC or FVTPL (Deloitte & Touche GmbH Wirtschaftsprüfungsgesellschaft 2014, 15).

Nevertheless, IFRS 9.4.2.1 (a)-(d) list the exceptions for which the FVTPL needs to be used. First of all, it affects financial liabilities held for trading, derivatives showing a negative FV and all financial liabilities for which the FVO is exercised. Secondly, it includes financial liabilities resulting from a transmission of financial assets. Consequently, financial liabilities are measured at FVTPL in case a write-off is not possible or the liability is intended for a continuing involvement. Therefore, IFRS 9.3.2.15 and IFRS 9.3.2.17 set special arrangements regarding the measurement. The third exception are financial guarantee contracts. These contracts are measured at the higher amount for the initial recognition applying IAS 37 or IAS 18, respectively. Furthermore, the guarantor is obliged to pay a fixed amount if losses occur due to the guaranteed debt instrument. Finally, the FVTPL is applied to loan commitments set below the market interest rate. The measurement is conducted equally as for financial guarantee contracts (Deloitte & Touche GmbH Wirtschaftsprüfungsgesellschaft 2011, 36).

In regard to the FVO, the possibility to opt in is still as it was defined in IAS 39. By applying the FVO, accounting mismatches are eliminated. Further, financial assets respectively financial liabilities are grouped according to the risk strategy or investment strategy in order to analyse the development of the FV. The results are usually communicated to key positions within the company such as the management and the supervisory board (Deloitte & Touche GmbH Wirtschaftsprüfungsgesellschaft 2011, 37).

While the separation of the derivative from the host contract is not required for financial assets, financial liabilities are treated differently. Therefore, an embedded derivative is split from the host contract as under IAS 39. The separation also impacts the measurement. While the embedded derivative is measured at FVTPL, the host contract is measured at AC for which the effective interest rate method is applied (Sagerschnig 2016, 11f).

The separation of an embedded derivative and the host contract is required if one of three conditions are met. First of all, the separation is conducted for embedded derivatives that are not closely linked to the economical characteristics and risks of the host contract. Secondly, if an independent instrument shows the same contract conditions as the derivative and thirdly, if the structured product is not measured at FV (Deloitte & Touche GmbH Wirtschaftsprüfungsgesellschaft 2011, 37f.).

Additionally, the new amendments affect the FVO in regard to the financial liabilities. The relevant aspect of the FVO before the alteration is the deterioration of the own financial standing and the influence on the rating. However, this decrease would still result in an income in the P & L. In accordance with IFRS 9.5.7.7 financial liabilities measured at FV are captured in the P & L and the change in the FV occurred through the own creditworthiness is recorded under the OCI which is adjusted by equity (Sagerschnig 2016, 10).

The IASB decided to adjust the previously applied approach in order to avoid effects on the income temporarily. This was due to the fact that solely a scheduled redemption results in the rebooking of income which initially is attributable to the deterioration of the own creditworthiness. Nevertheless, this separation into the P & L and OCI is only allowed for the own creditworthiness unless an accounting mismatch evolves, otherwise all changes in the FV are recorded in the P & L. Therefore, other financial instruments measured at FVTPL are not intended for the OCI such as financial liabilities held for trading and derivatives as well as financial guarantee contracts and loan commitments (Deloitte & Touche GmbH Wirtschaftsprüfungsgesellschaft 2011, 39ff.).

Once the change in the own creditworthiness is recorded in the OCI, a reclassification to the P & L is not allowed even if the financial liability is written off. The amounts booked in the OCI may be reclassified into the equity as accumulated other comprehensive income if required instead. As the change of the own creditworthiness reflects the default risk, it is necessary to distinguish this risk from the settlement risk regarding financial assets. The default risk is the risk of the contracting party not meeting the obligations regarding the financial instrument. As a result, the other contracting party might face a loss. In contrast, the settlement risk arises if the financial liability is either linked to the financial asset through contractual terms or its value depends on the financial asset due to a ring-fencing (Deloitte & Touche GmbH Wirtschafts-prüfungsgesellschaft 2011, 39).

Furthermore, the highlight on the own creditworthiness is considered as the residual amount which cannot be traced back to market changes. Consequently, unfavourable changes in the market such as the reference interest rate, prices of financial instruments of other companies or commodity prices are booked into the P & L (Deloitte & Touche GmbH Wirtschaftsprüfungsgesellschaft 2011, 39).

In case the FV of the financial liability solely changes due to the market risk or rather the movement of the market interest rate, it is advisable to determine the residual amount caused by the own creditworthiness applying the standard approach. As a result, the credit spread is described as the FV at time zero and the contractual cash flows are considered in order to set the return from which the reference interest rate is subtracted and leads to the credit spread for the instrument. Afterwards, the contractual cash flows are divided by the sum of credit spread for the instrument and the reference interest rate resulting in the present value of the contractual cash flows. Finally, the change in the own credit spread is determined as the difference between the FV and present value of the previously calculated contractual cash flows (Deloitte & Touche GmbH Wirtschaftsprüfungsgesellschaft 2011, 39f.).

Furthermore, reporting duties are more demanding and detailed. The disclosures on financial instruments stated in IFRS 7 are adapted to the new standards of IFRS 9. The main enhancements are made for financial liabilities regarding the FV in accordance to IFRS 7.10-11. and financial assets in terms of the FVOCI. Additionally, reporting duties are widened in case if the business model changes e.g. the change regarding the timing, the amount and the occasion for the change to the new business model (Sagerschnig 2016, 12).

3.2.2 Phase II – Amortised Cost and Impairment

The second phase of IFRS 9 deals with amortised costs and impairments. The reason for the renewed standards can be traced back to the incurred loss model of the IAS 39. Due to the usage of this model, impairments for loans are only recognised if there is a triggering event. Consequently, this approach favoured the extent of the financial crisis. In order to counteract this outcome, the new impairment model called the expected credit loss model (ECL) was introduced in 2014 as a part of IFRS 9 (Sagerschnig 2016, 12f.).

The ECL is applicable for financial assets which are measured at AC and FVOCI, loan commitments and financial guarantee contracts unless the measurement is at FVTPL, lease receivables in line with IFRS 17 as well as contract assets for which IFRS 15 is used (Deloitte & Touche GmbH Wirtschaftsprüfungsgesellschaft 2014, 16).

According to IFRS 9.B5.5.7 the previously required triggering event is not relevant anymore, consequently, the significance of the default risk is given despite changes in the creditworthiness or occurring defaults (Institut der Wirtschaftsprüfer 2018, 1793).

Moreover, the ECL implies a three-stage approach. Generally, financial instruments are categorised at stage one at the initial recognition. Furthermore, they belong to stage one if there is an internal rating. For stage one the loss allowance is determined by the 12-month expected credit loss. Further, the gross book value is required for the calculation of the interest income. However, stage two is applied if no internal rating exists for the financial instrument. Another circumstance are substantial changes in the amount due to the deterioration of creditworthiness in regard to the subsequent measurement. While the calculation of the interest income is equal to stage one, the 12-month expected credit losses are replaced by the lifetime expected credit losses. Consequently, during the remaining period of the financial instrument, the present value of the expected losses is evaluated (Deloitte & Touche GmbH Wirtschaftsprüfungsgesellschaft 2014, 16f.; Institut der Wirtschaftsprüfer 2018, 1625; Sagerschnig 2016, 15).

Finally, if the financial instrument is significantly affected by a default risk and an objective evidence for the impairment exists, the categorisation follows stage three of the ECL for which the lifetime expected credit losses are considered. In contrast to stage one and two, the interest income is calculated on the net book value (Deloitte & Touche GmbH Wirtschaftsprüfungsgesellschaft 2014, 17).

Additionally, the ECL is reviewed on the reporting date to assure that each financial instrument is appropriately categorised. The decisive factor for the switch between stage one and two is the probability of default (PD) for the outstanding period – also referred to as the lifetime PD. In order to distinguish between the stages, it is necessary to define the term default. While this task is assigned to the internal risk management of the company, it usually considers 90 days overdue. Additionally, a comparison between the PD at initial recognition and the PD at the reporting date is carried out to evaluate if a change in the default occurred. The extent to which it is possible, each financial instrument is evaluated separately. However, if real-time identification is not feasible, the review is carried out as a portfolio to avoid defaults in payment. Nevertheless, the above described approach is avoidable if the financial instrument is investment graded. In addition, the 12-month PD may be used if the lifetime PD is less relevant. Finally, financial instruments are transferred to stage two if contractual payments are 30 days overdue unless there is proof of insignificance (Deloitte & Touche GmbH Wirtschaftsprüfungsgesellschaft 2014, 17f.).

In regard to the reporting date, a financial instrument categorised into stage two is transferred to stage three due to objective evidence of impairment. A few objective evidence are for instance financial difficulties faced by the debtor, breach of agreement related to a default payment, the possibility to become insolvent or face a restructuring process. Moreover, accounts receivables, lease receivables and contract assets are automatically categorised into stage two, thereby requiring the application of the lifetime expected credit losses. While a transfer to stage three in case of an objective evidence of impairment is mandatory, downgrading to stage one is not allowed. Nevertheless, if there is an objective evidence of impairment for the financial instrument, the expected instead of the contractual cash flows are taken into account. Further, the expected loss at the initial recognition is used and changes are solely booked into the P & L for the remaining time (Deloitte & Touche GmbH Wirtschaftsprüfungsgesellschaft 2014, 19f.).

In order to estimate the expected loss, several aspects are considered. First of all, all available information including those from the past, present and the future are relevant. The information used refers not only to the debtor but also to economic factors. Secondly, the expected cash flows are relevant for the definition of the expected loss. For the calculation of the expected loss, the present value of the expected cash flow on the one hand and the income which results from selling securities on the other hand is subtracted from the present value of the contractual cash flows. Furthermore, a scenario analysis is applied to determine the expected value. Consequently, the expected value is illustrated with or without default. In addition, the discount factor is dependent on the financial instrument. Generally, the calculation of the effective interest rate differs for fixed and variable interest rates. For fixed income instruments, the effective interest rate equals the discount rate used for the present value at initial recognition. In contrast to that, the effective interest rate for an instrument with variable interest is set by the current effective interest rate. The calculation requests parameters such as the PD, exposure at default (EAD) and the loss given default (LGD), however, credit loss rates are also considered to estimate the expected loss in regard to the 12-month expected credit losses. It is important to point out that the 12-month expected credit losses is not the loss in the next twelve months but rather corresponds to the expected loss for the outstanding time and a PD in the next twelve months (Deloitte & Touche GmbH Wirtschaftsprüfungsgesellschaft 2014, 20f.).

3.2.3 Phase III – Hedge Accounting

Finally, the third phase of IFRS 9 discusses the topic of hedge accounting which was published in November 2013. One of the objectives is to connect hedge accounting to the risk strategy of the company. As a result, the objective set in IFRS 9.6.1.1 considers hedge accounting as a feature in the risk management and aims to manage exposures which could impact the P & L. Therefore, risk management that carries out hedges intends to illustrate the effect on the financial instruments used. Due to that, the traceability between risk management and hedge accounting has been improved (Institut der Wirtschaftsprüfer 2018, 1639; Sagerschnig 2016, 18f.).

However, hedge accounting is only permitted if the prerequisites are met. In accordance with IFRS 9.6.4.1 both a hedge instrument and hedge item must be eligible in order to generate a hedge relationship. Furthermore, a documentation of the procedure and designation of hedge instrument and hedge item is requested. Additionally, the risks which are intended be hedged, the risk management strategy and the effectiveness of the hedge must be described. In contrast to IAS 39, the focus of IFRS 9 are set on the risk management and its objective which consequently might result in the termination of a hedge relationship in case risk management is affected negatively (Institut der Wirtschaftsprüfer 2018, 1645 and 1647; Sagerschnig 2016, 19).

A further amendment in this phase is non-derivative financial instruments used as a hedge instrument under the condition that it is categorised as FVTPL. However, there is one exception in regard to non-derivative financial liabilities measured at FVTPL in accordance to IFRS 9.6.2.2. With respect to the classification and measurement in phase one, changes in the own creditworthiness are booked in the OCI whereas the residual amount is transferred into the P & L. Due to the consideration of the OCI and P & L, the financial instrument cannot be classified as hedge instrument as the change is not considered entirely in the P & L (Deloitte & Touche GmbH Wirtschaftsprüfungsgesellschaft 2014, 22; Institut der Wirtschaftsprüfer 2018, 1641; Sagerschnig 2016, 20).

In terms of the hedged item, IFRS 9 allow to group non-derivative and derivative financial instruments as exposure. Further, IFRS 9.6.3.1 categorise recorded assets and liabilities, unrecognised firm commitments, transactions to be carried out with a high probability or net investments as hedge instrument (Deloitte & Touche GmbH Wirtschaftsprüfungsgesellschaft 2014, 22; Institut der Wirtschaftsprüfer 2018, 1643; Sagerschnig 2016, 20).

With the introduction of IFRS 9, changes are made in regard to the hedge effectiveness. While IAS 39 requested the hedge effectiveness to be ranged between 80 % and 125 %, IFRS 9.6.4.1(c) require an economical connection between the hedge item and hedge instrument, the credit risk not to significantly affect the hedge relationship and a documentation of the hedge ratio (Deloitte & Touche GmbH Wirtschaftsprüfungsgesellschaft 2014, 22; Institut der Wirtschaftsprüfer 2018, 1645 and 1647; Sagerschnig 2016, 20).

Furthermore, if the hedge relationship shows a hedge ineffectiveness although the aim of the risk management remains unchanged, IFRS 9.6.5.5 state that the hedge ratio and the hedge relationship need to be adapted. In contrast to this approach of rebalancing in IFRS 9, IAS 39 required the termination and the correct designation of the hedge relationship (Institut der Wirtschaftsprüfer 2018, 1649; Sagerschnig 2016, 21).

With respect to the cut-off of hedge relationships, the option to voluntary discontinue the hedge relationship is not provided anymore. In fact, the hedge relationship stops if the adaption is not carried out or if there is an expiration, termination or sale in accordance with IFRS 9.6.5.6 (Institut der Wirtschaftsprüfer 2018, 1649; Sagerschnig 2016, 21).

Due to the changes, IFRS 7 and its disclosure requirements needed an enhancement. IFRS 7.21A describe relevant aspects regarding the topic of risk management strategy and risks involved. While IFRS 7.22B-22C focus on the quantitative characteristics such as the influence of hedging on future cash flows, IFRS 7.24A-24F summarise the effect of hedge accounting for the financial positions (Institut der Wirtschaftsprüfer 2018, 1485ff. and 1491ff.; Sagerschnig 2016, 22).

3.3 Valuation, classification and measurement under IFRS 9 and IAS 39

With regards to the main amendments, this paper also describes the general valuation principles as well as classification and measurement of financial instruments on the asset and liability sides. Due to the fact that IFRS 9 affect basically almost the same area of application as IAS 39 except for the changes made, this chapter provides a compromised overview of the balance sheet items. Furthermore, applying IFRS 9, IAS 32 dealing with the presentation and IFRS 7 stating the disclosure of financial instruments are of relevance for creating annual reports (PricewaterhouseCoopers Aktiengesellschaft Wirtschaftsprüfungsgesellschaft 2017a, 1031).

3.3.1 Financial Assets

To begin with, a financial asset is solely recorded if it is part of a contractual agreement in accordance with IFRS 9.3.1.1. For this case, IFRS 9.B3.1.2 list examples to meet this requirement. A contract evolves for instance from a legal obligation, respectively right for the owner or a firm commitment, where one party already fulfilled the contract. However, IAS 32.13 emphasise that writtenness is not requested unless an economic relationship legally exists between the parties. Regarding the date of recognition or derecognition in the

17

financial statement, IFRS 9.B3.1.3. set for regular way purchase or sale, the option for either the trade or settlement date. Compared to that, a forward contract is recorded or booked when the contract is concluded and loans are drawn up on the settlement date (PricewaterhouseCoopers Aktiengesellschaft Wirtschaftsprüfungsgesellschaft 2017a, 1037ff.; Wagenhofer 2018, 193 and 502f. and 535f.).

Neither the recognition nor the derecognition changed significantly as most parts regulated in IAS 39 were transferred to IFRS 9. First of all, financial assets are only derecognised for consolidated accounts in accordance with IFRS 9.3.2.1 as the financial asset might not be derecognised but rather transferred to a sub-company, consequently, it is still within the affiliated group. In order to determine the expiration date for the right to receive cash flows, a multilevel process is introduced. Especially financial instruments are possibly split into single parts or they are bundled as portfolio leading to the complexity in the derecognition. As a result, the multilevel process defines three steps: the economical approach, the risk and reward approach and the control concept. Prior to the transfer of financial assets to third parties, it is essential to evaluate if the financial asset in total or solely parts of it are derecognised. Assuming the financial asset is partly derecognised, IFRS 9.3.2.2. prescribe for the derecognition one of three criteria to be fulfilled. As a result, the cash flows of a part of the financial asset are either generated from the financial asset directly or result by a proportional share. Moreover, the cash flows of the proportional share must be entirely traceable back to the financial asset. However, the criteria are applicable to financial assets that are grouped. Unless one of the three criteria is met, the derecognition affects the financial asset in total (PricewaterhouseCoopers Aktiengesellschaft Wirtschaftsprüfungsgesellschaft 2017a, 1039ff.; Wagenhofer 2018, 503).

In regard to IFRS 9.3.2.3 a financial asset is derecognised at the expiration of the contractual rights to cash flows. This circumstance occurs for instance if the loan is repaid, an option is abandoned or one of the three criteria is fulfilled which leads to the derecognition of a part of the financial asset. Moreover, derecognition is carried out for the transfer of contractual cash flows or the distribution of cash flows to recipients, however, the primary owner remains to hold the contractual right to receive the cash flows. The latter, however, prescribes three conditions as stated in IFRS 9.3.2.5 to be met. First, there is an obligation for the primary owner to pay the cash flows based upon the right to initially receive the cash flows. Further, allowance is provided for advance payments for a short-term. Secondly, the financial asset cannot be sold or pledged unless it is for the purpose of assuring the payments to the recipients. Finally, the entity must provide payment without delay (PricewaterhouseCoopers Aktiengesellschaft Wirtschaftsprüfungsgesellschaft 2017a, 1039 and 1041; Wagenhofer 2018, 504).

After conducting the economical approach, the risk and reward approach is relevant for reviewing a derecognition. Under the condition that IFRS 9.3.2.4(a) are fulfilled, consequently, the contractual right of receiving cash flows is transferred, the risk and reward approach requires examining whether risk and reward of the financial instrument are also essentially transferred in accordance with IFRS 9.3.2.6(a). Consequently, the measurement and effect on the present value of the net cash flows is carried out with risks e.g. interest rate risk, exchange risk and default risk and once without any risk factors. Thereby, it can be shown if risks impact the result using the current market interest rate. According to IFRS 9.3.2.7 a financial asset is transferred if the fluctuations resulting from the risk factors are not significant anymore. Nevertheless, the IASB does not set a predefined range for determining significance (PricewaterhouseCoopers Aktiengesellschaft Wirtschaftsprüfungsgesellschaft 2017a, 1041f.; Wagenhofer 2018, 504f.).

Consequently, the control concept in terms of the economic approach might be used unless the risk and reward approach indicates a finding. In case of such an occurrence, it is necessary to distinguish if the transfer of control stays with the primary owner or the recipient. In fact, if the recipient owns control, a derecognition comes into force in accordance with IFRS 9.B3.2.7, otherwise the financial asset is kept and accounted for due to a continuing involvement. However, the last approach to determine whether derecognition is feasible, is the so-called pass through test which in turn still requires the risk and reward approach. As a result, a financial asset is derecognised, not derecognised or held as continuing involvement (PricewaterhouseCoopers Aktiengesellschaft Wirtschaftsprüfungsgesellschaft 2017a, 1042ff.; Wagenhofer 2018, 538).

Furthermore, a financial asset, especially financial instruments, and its conditions may be adapted afterwards. Modifications are attributable to market changes e.g. the market interest rate or creditworthiness which contribute to a prolongation of the term or the forbearance of interest payments. In terms of the new standards, IFRS 9 introduced substantial and unsubstantial modifications, while the latter is not being derecognised. In accordance with IFRS 9.3.2.3(a) in connection with IFRS 9.B5.5.25 the original financial asset is derecognised and recognised as financial asset including the significant modification. However, quantitative and qualitative analyses are necessary to evaluate if the re-recognition is necessary. While the former is recommended for numerousness modifications applying a present value comparison, the latter is simpler as the result is shown clearly, for instance the arrangement to change a currency (PricewaterhouseCoopers Aktiengesellschaft Wirtschaftsprüfungs-gesellschaft 2017a, 1045ff.; Wagenhofer 2018, 503 and 573).

As already described, a financial asset is recognised according to IFRS 9.3.1.1, which also includes the topics of initial categorisation and measurement. A financial asset is categorised in regard to the business model and contractual cash flows, also called the SPPI-criterion which means "Solely Payments of

Principal and Interest". However, the decision made regarding classification and measurement is determined by the requirements of IFRS 9. In terms of the business model, three possible options exist: hold and collect, hold and sell or a third classification is provided, which is neither hold and collect nor hold and sell but can be rather considered as a business model for residuals. Nevertheless, IFRS 9.B4.1.2 define that the classification is not carried out for each financial instrument instead financial instruments are set into groups following an objective. As a result, a company might define different business models which affect all three options and include portfolios or sub-portfolios of financial instruments. In connection with the business model and its definition, IAS 24 regarding related party disclosures is of relevance due to the fact that key positions set the objectives. Moreover, it is requested to evaluate and review the business model as well as the performance and reporting of the financial instruments. This also includes risks which have to be dealt with or the compensation of managers according to IFRS 9.B4.1.2B. Further, there is an additional requirement for the business model hold to collect. As stated in IFRS 9.B4.1.2C it is required to determine frequency, amount, the time of previous sales and to estimate the development in this area for the future. It is notable that the management of financial instruments and the objective to achieve cash flows is referred to as hold and collect, while hold and sell reflects the sale of financial assets (Deloitte & Touche GmbH Wirtschaftsprüfungsgesellschaft 2011, 6; PricewaterhouseCoopers Aktiengesellschaft Wirtschaftsprüfungsgesellschaft 2017a, 1057f.; Wagenhofer 2018, 502 and 546f.).

Before each classification is described, it is necessary to explain the business model and the SPPI-criterion in detail. The business model hold to collect is highly oriented to hold the financial instrument until it matures. In fact, this is also a requirement for the categorisation. However, this approach differs from IAS 39 as the held-to-maturity classification requires the financial instrument to be reclassified if it is not held until it matures. In contrast to that, IFRS 9.B4.1.3 allow to hold and collect financial instruments even if it is not held until maturity. Such a circumstance might evolve from a deterioration of the creditworthiness eventually breaching the guidelines of investing set by the management (IFRS 9.B4.1.3A) or if the sale is executed close to the maturity (IFRS 9.B4.1.3B) (PricewaterhouseCoopers Aktiengesellschaft Wirtschaftsprüfungsgesellschaft 2017a, 1061f.; Wagenhofer 2018, 547).

However, from time to time there might be a need for unexpected sales for other reasons than the creditworthiness or the execution date. Due to that, unexpected sales for the business model hold to collect are only permitted if it is an irregular sale with even a significant amount or is a sale with an insignificant amount and executed often in accordance with IFRS 9.B4.1.3B. Those exceptions as determined in IFRS 9.B4.1.4 are for instance controlling currency or credit risk due to a stress scenario or reducing risk weighted assets to meet the requirements set in the Capital Requirements Regulation (CRR). However, IFRS 9 set no clear definition of irregular sales but usually require thresholds in regard to the frequency in practice. Nevertheless, it is reasonable to consider cases that tend to last for a long period (PricewaterhouseCoopers Aktiengesellschaft Wirtschaftsprüfungsgesellschaft 2017a, 1063f.; Wagenhofer 2018, 547ff.).

Furthermore, if it is neither an irregular nor an insignificant sale, it might be necessary to review the initial business model and restate errors retrospectively according to IAS 8. In contrast to that, a financial asset, a part of it or the entire portfolio is reclassified in accordance with IFRS 9.B4.4.1 under the condition that the requirements are met. Finally, sales regarding the business model hold to collect are subject to disclosure requirements as stated in IFRS 7.20A (PricewaterhouseCoopers Aktiengesellschaft Wirtschaftsprüfungsgesellschaft 2017a, 1065f.; Wagenhofer 2018, 68f. and 565f. and 465).

In addition to the business model hold to collect, IFRS 9.B4.1.2A also mention the business model hold to sell under the condition that all information available is considered for the classification. In line with IFRS 9.B4.1.4Aff. the management sets this business model if it aims to hold and sell financial assets in order to control liquidity on a daily basis or to adjust the maturity of financial assets to financial liabilities maximising the yield. In contrast to the business model hold to collect, hold to sell initially causes a high frequency and thus an increased amount of sales. As in the previous cases, also hold to sell is not explicitly defined in IFRS 9 regarding its threshold (PricewaterhouseCoopers Aktiengesellschaft Wirtschaftsprüfungsgesellschaft 2017a, 1066ff.; Wagenhofer 2018, 546 and 549ff.).

Finally, the business model for residuals as its name implies includes financial assets which are neither hold to collect nor hold to sell. As a result, the measurement is at FVTPL and is relevant for the management concerning the purchase and sale of financial assets or a portfolio in accordance with IFRS 9.B4.1.5 and IFRS 9.B4.1.6 (PricewaterhouseCoopers Aktiengesellschaft Wirtschaftsprüfungsgesellschaft 2017a, 1069; Wagenhofer 2018, 551f.).

Another aspect to consider is the contractual cash flow, also considered as SPPI test. Consequently, solely the payment of principal and interest on the principal amount outstanding are conditions in order to pass the SPPI test as stated in IFRS 9.B4.1.7. Each financial instrument is examined at the initial recognition regarding the fulfilment of the SPPI test and considers possible contract terms for the future. In regard to the principal, IFRS 9.B4.1.7B describe the principal as FV of the financial asset. However, the FV also reflects changes which are traceable back to repayments. Moreover, the FV is set equal to the acquisition costs. Referring to the interest, IFRS 9.4.1.3(b) and IFRS 9.B4.1.7A list the acceptable interest components for the contractual cash flow condition. Due to the credit arrangement, the time value of the money and the resulting default risk, credit risks such as liquidity risk, administration costs and the profit margin are named as fees in terms of interest components. Moreover, further risks resulting from the credit arrangement affecting the parties are not included as interest components, for instance the risk of price changes in terms of raw materials or equity securities. The contractual cash flow condition is reviewed on an individual basis, however, the financial asset may be categorised into the business model for residuals or is designated as a FVO according to IFRS 9.4.1.1 respectively IFRS 9.4.1.5 (PricewaterhouseCoopers Aktiengesellschaft Wirtschaftsprüfungsgesellschaft 2017a, 1074f. and 1076 and 1079; Wagenhofer 2018, 507f. and 552).

Furthermore, the contractual cash flow condition is not affected by a financial instrument for which a functional currency is chosen (IFRS 9.B4.1.8). In addition, the exchange rate on the date of payment is applied in order to guarantee that the SPPI criterion is achieved. However, few exceptions which are not conform with the contractual cash flow condition exist. As in IFRS 9.B4.1.9 financial instruments that fail the SPPI test are those that focus on leverage, e.g. options, forward contracts or swap contracts (PricewaterhouseCoopers Aktiengesellschaft Wirtschaftsprüfungsgesellschaft 2017a, 1075; Wagenhofer 2018, 552).

Moreover, there are a few examples that are described shortly in regard to the SPPI requirement. For instance a debt instrument which yields a floating interest rate (IFRS 9.B4.1.11(a)) fulfils the contractual cash flow condition demanding e.g. a fee for the time value and a profit margin assuming the 3-month Euro Interbank Offered Rate (EURIBOR) and the interest rate adjustment of 3 months at a fixed maturity (IFRS 9.B4.1.13). In contrast to that, inverse floating rates breach the contractual cash flow condition. Nevertheless, a gradually growing interest unless it includes optional interest rate adjustments and interest payments in arrear are conform with the contractual cash flow. In accordance to IFRS 9.4.1.3(b) and IFRS 9.B4.1.7A zero coupon bonds are required to fulfil the SPPI criterion and provide an interest rate which is in line with the market calculated as the difference between the issuing price and amount repaid. However, as soon as the interest payment is related to the annual returns or in case the repayment of the principal is postponed or temporarily abandoned and neither principal payment nor interest is paid on, then the contractual cash flow is not met (PricewaterhouseCoopers Aktiengesellschaft Wirtschaftsprüfungs-gesellschaft 2017a, 1079ff.; Wagenhofer 2018, 508 and 552 and 554ff.).

Regarding the time value of money, it is necessary to conduct a benchmark test for the contractual cash flow condition as the time value cannot compensate risks directly in connection to financial instruments according to IFRS 9.B4.1.9B. In general, the time value is under certain conditions permitted to be modified considering the SPPI criterion. As prescribed in IFRS 9.B4.1.9B-E a modification is the monthly adjustment of the interest rate based on the 12-month-EURIBOR. While the qualitative or quantitative analysis might be advisable to determine principal and interest payments, the benchmark is another option. The approach of the benchmark test is to find a similar financial instrument equipped with the same contractual terms and default risk. Consequently, the modified contractual cash flow is permitted for use if a deviation exists between the undiscounted cash flows of the financial asset intended for classification and the financial asset used as benchmark. However, this decision is not solely influenced by the current but also the future situation. Therefore, the duration of the financial assets and probable scenarios which might affect the SPPI criterion are taken into account (PricewaterhouseCoopers Aktiengesellschaft Wirtschaftsprüfungs-gesellschaft 2017a, 1085f.; Wagenhofer 2018, 552f.).

Besides the modification of the time value, the contractual cash flows may also be adapted in regard to the conditional contractual terms, e.g. the timing and amount. The standards for this circumstance are described in IFRS 9.B4.1.10 and require the examination of the SPPI criterion before and after the adaption. Furthermore, a trigger event needs to be considered. The SPPI criterion is met for instance if the interest rate rises as the debtor fails to repay on the date settled which initially results in a default risk. In contrast to that, the increase of the interest rate related to a market index violates the SPPI criterion. However, the linkage to an inflation rate of the respective currency – e.g. the harmonised index of consumer prices – is permitted as long as no leverage is generated. Moreover, conditional contractual terms allowed are caps, floors and collars. In addition, IFRS 9.B4.1.11(b) state that an early repayment respectively the dismissal is allowed if the amount left reflects solely the payment of the principal and interest, thereby requiring a prepayment fee. This approach is reversely used for the prolongation of a contract (PricewaterhouseCoopers Aktiengesellschaft Wirtschaftsprüfungsgesellschaft 2017a, 1089ff. and 1093f.; Wagenhofer 2018, 553ff.).

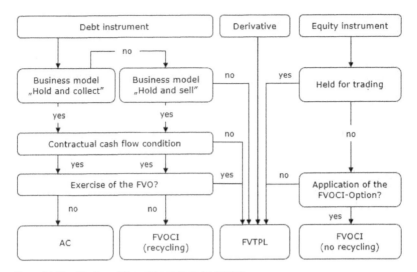

Figure 1 | Classification of financial assets under IFRS 9

(Source: PricewaterhouseCoopers Aktiengesellschaft Wirtschaftsprüfungsgesellschaft 2017a, 1056)

As shown in the graph above, the decision tree leads to the classification of the
financial asset based on its characteristics such as the differentiation between
debt instrument, derivatives and equity instruments but also in terms of
business model, contractual cash flow terms as well as held for trading. IFRS 9
define three respectively four classification categories which influence the
subsequent measurement of the financial asset. In accordance with IFRS
9.4.1.2(a) in connection with IFRS 9.B4.1.2C a financial asset is measured at
AC based on the condition that the business model is hold to collect and the
contractual cash flow condition meets the requirement of solely principal and
interest payments (IFRS 9.4.1.2(b) and IFRS 9.B4.1.7). An example for this
categorisation is loans and bonds (PricewaterhouseCoopers Aktiengesellschaft
Wirtschaftsprüfungsgesellschaft 2017a, 1051f. and 1056; Wagenhofer 2018,
507f. and 547 and 552).

In contrast to that, if a financial asset belongs to the business model hold to sell
(IFRS 9.4.1.2A(a) and IFRS 9.B4.1.4A) and fulfils the contractual cash flow
condition (IFRS 9.4.1.2A(b) and IFRS 9.B4.1.7), then the measurement is
carried out at FVOCI. In this case, the FVOCI measurement is mandatory with
recycling. Therefore, changes in the FV are recorded in the OCI while other
changes are booked in the P & L (PricewaterhouseCoopers Aktiengesellschaft
Wirtschaftsprüfungsgesellschaft 2017a, 1053f.; Wagenhofer 2018, 508 and
549f. and 552).

Furthermore, an equity instrument which is not held for trading, is measured at FVOCI without recycling unless the decision is made to opt in for the FVO in accordance with IFRS 9.5.7.5. Additionally, once designated at FVOCI, the decision is irrevocable. Finally, financial assets are measured at FVTPL if neither the business model nor the contractual cash flow condition is met. Moreover, exercising the FVO, derivatives, equity instruments held for trading respectively those who are not opting in for the FVOCI option result in the measurement at FVTPL (PricewaterhouseCoopers Aktiengesellschaft Wirtschaftsprüfungsgesellschaft 2017a, 1053f.; Wagenhofer 2018, 515).

In terms of exercising the FVO, it must be considered that this right – once designated – the decision is irrevocable and its prerequisite is the occurrence of an accounting mismatch which is consequently lessened by applying the measurement at FVTPL according to IFRS 9.4.1.5. As described in IFRS 9.B4.1.30(b) a financial asset or liability might face the same risk, e.g. interest rate risk and therefore a designation favours the offsetting (PricewaterhouseCoopers Aktiengesellschaft Wirtschaftsprüfungsgesellschaft 2017a, 1055; Wagenhofer 2018, 508 and 561).

Financial assets are permitted in contrast to financial liabilities for reclassification. In terms of the circumstance for a reclassification, IFRS 9.4.4.1 state that financial assets are reclassified if the business model changes. Nevertheless, such a decision is to be concluded by the management and occurs if there a significant and influencing conditions. While changing the business model occurs relatively rarely, it is still possible in case the company purchases another company splitting the management of loans from hold to sell to hold to collect. Moreover, the change in the business model results from abandoning or gathering a new business segment which substantially influences the business model in accordance with IFRS 9.B4.4.1. In addition, the reclassification is only carried out after the business model has been adapted (IFRS 9.B4.4.2) (PricewaterhouseCoopers Aktiengesellschaft Wirtschaftsprüfungsgesellschaft 2017a, 1109ff.; Wagenhofer 2018, 510 and 565f.).

However, IFRS 9.B4.4.3 set exceptions for the reclassification. Therefore, single financial assets even if significant changes evolve, are not intended for reclassification. Furthermore, temporarily illiquid markets or a transfer within the company of a financial asset leave the business model unaffected. In fact, previously designated hedge instruments that are to be designated in terms of cash flow and net investment hedges are excluded from the business model amendment, hence also from the reclassification according to IFRS 9.4.4.3. Additionally, the change in the cash flow condition or a modification carried out regarding the contractual terms do not lead to a reclassification (PricewaterhouseCoopers Aktiengesellschaft Wirtschaftsprüfungsgesellschaft 2017a, 1111f.; Wagenhofer 2018, 510 and 566).

Under the assumption that a reclassification is conducted and the conditions are met, the financial asset is assigned a different category and measurement unless the FVO is exercised which results in an irrevocable designation in accordance with IFRS 9.4.1.5. The reclassification of FVTPL, FVOCI and AC leads to fewer adaptions. Beginning with FVTPL and FVOCI to be reclassified as AC, IFRS 9.5.6.3 require the FV on the day of the reclassification to be recognised as the gross book value. As a result, the difference between the gross book value and the amount to be repaid is continually amortised applying the effective interest rate. Secondly, reclassifying from FVTPL to FVOCI and vice versa does not impact the FV. Nevertheless, the profit and loss booked in the OCI is requested to be reclassified leading to the offsetting in the P & L instead of the equity. In contrast to that, reclassifying FVTPL to FVOCI requires FV changes to be booked in the OCI. Finally, reclassification from AC to FVTPL requires for the recognition the FV. Consequently, the difference between the AC and FV are booked into the P & L (IFRS 9.5.6.2). Similarly, the change from AC to FVOCI requires the difference between the AC and FV to be recorded in the OCI in accordance with IFRS 9.5.6.4 (PricewaterhouseCoopers Aktiengesellschaft Wirtschaftsprüfungsgesellschaft 2017a, 1113ff.; Wagenhofer 2018, 508 and 514).

Upon deciding on the classification category, the next step is the measurement in regard to the initial recognition. Generally, as applied in IAS 39, every financial asset and liability is measured at FV in accordance with IFRS 9.5.1.1. The FV is under IFRS 13.9 the price on the measurement date for market participants to sell or transfer a financial asset or liability considering that it occurs as regular transaction. Further, the price is observed on the primary or any other favourable market allowing to undertake a transaction regardless whether prices are observable or require estimation via measurement technics (IFRS 13.24). Additionally, transaction costs which occur through the purchase or sale of the financial asset or liability are added to or subtracted from the initial costs. However, this is not applicable to the classification at FVTPL both for financial assets and liabilities (PricewaterhouseCoopers Aktiengesellschaft Wirtschaftsprüfungsgesellschaft 2017a, 1117 and 1239.; Wagenhofer 2018, 510 and 668f.)

In terms of the transaction costs, IFRS 9 include the same content as IAS 39. As prescribed in IFRS 9.B5.4.8, transaction costs are considered as fees and commissions charged by intermediaries, consultants, agents and brokers as well as fees and taxes paid to regulators and securities market. Moreover, this paragraph also lists items which are not recognised as transaction costs such as disagio/agio, costs of financing and other costs occurring within the company in regard to management and administration (PricewaterhouseCoopers Aktiengesellschaft Wirtschaftsprüfungsgesellschaft 2017a, 1117f.; Wagenhofer 2018, 569).

In accordance with IFRS 9.B5.1.1 the FV is at the initial recognition equal to the transaction costs. However, the transaction costs might include costs not traceable back to the financial instruments. As a result, the FV is to be determined by the company itself. In terms of loans or accounts receivables without an interest rate, IFRS 9 set the approach for determining the FV by using similar instruments. Thus, depending on the rating of a similar instrument, the cash flows are discounted by the market interest rate also considering currency, maturity and other factors. In fact, amounts borrowed afterwards are treated as expenses (PricewaterhouseCoopers Aktiengesellschaft Wirtschaftsprüfungsgesellschaft 2017a, 1117f.; Wagenhofer 2018, 566).

One main difference between IAS 39 and IFRS 9 is the topic credit impairments and the measurement of financial instruments at the initial recognition. Consequently, credit impairments used to be prohibited and only intended for the subsequent measurement in IAS 39 whereas IFRS 9 allow credit impairments at the initial recognition. Furthermore, loan commitments and forward loan-contracts need to be distinguished from those loan commitments in IFRS 9.2.3. While the former is regulated in IAS 37, the latter belongs to IFRS 9. Nevertheless, loan commitments paid out are recognised using IFRS 9 (PricewaterhouseCoopers Aktiengesellschaft Wirtschaftsprüfungsgesellschaft 2017a, 1118f.; Wagenhofer 2018, 501f.).

Another relevant aspect for the measurement at initial recognition is securities. Due to the fact that securities are bought at different prices, the evaluation of the initial costs depends on the measurement of either the separate valuation of a security or the aggregation of a type of security. Therefore, IAS 2 which deals with inventories is applied for assessing the initial cost. The approaches used are first in – first out (FIFO), average and the classification based upon individual decisions. Using the average approach on all securities is less cumbersome and if turnover ratios are high, the average price is calculated more frequently (PricewaterhouseCoopers Aktiengesellschaft Wirtschaftsprüfungs-gesellschaft 2017a, 580f. and 1119).

Furthermore, the measurement at initial recognition is influenced by regular way contracts. When a contract is concluded, the financial instrument is recorded in the balance sheet. However, for regular way contracts a time span between the trade and settlement date is considered. Consequently, if a trade date is not equal to the settlement date, the transaction is seen as derivative but not accounted for as long as it remains a regular way contract fulfilling commercial usage in terms of the time span. In accordance with IFRS 9.3.1.2, a regular way contract is allowed to be accounted for on either the trade date or on the settlement date. However, once the decision is made, an alteration is not permitted. Nevertheless, the trade or the settlement date is decided on each classification category enabling more flexibility (IFRS 9.B3.1.3) (PricewaterhouseCoopers Aktiengesellschaft Wirtschaftsprüfungsgesellschaft 2017a, 1119f.; Wagenhofer 2018, 502f. and 535).

The decision made between the trade date and the settlement date impacts accounting. The trade date as described in IFRS B.3.1.5 require the buyer to record the asset and liability for the payment on the trade date. In contrast to that, the seller of the asset is requested to derecognise the asset and realise a profit or loss occurring due to the transaction as well as the recording of the receivable on the trade date. Regarding the settlement date, which is the date when the asset is delivered, the procedure is similar. Therefore, the asset is recognised on the settlement date whereas the derecognition considering profit and losses is carried out on the settlement date. However, deciding for the settlement date also results in the realisation of FV changes during the trade and settlement date. According to IFRS 9.B3.1.6, changes are booked to the P & L respectively to the OCI in regard to the classification category, whereas AC is not impacted (PricewaterhouseCoopers Aktiengesellschaft Wirtschafts-prüfungsgesellschaft 2017a, 1120f.; Wagenhofer 2018, 535f.).

The final topic described in this chapter is the subsequent measurement of financial assets. In accordance with IFRS 9.5.2.1, the subsequent measurement considers AC, FVOCI and FVTPL reflecting also the classification categories at the initial recognition. With reference to figure one (classification of financial assets), the subsequent measurement of debt instruments follows AC, FVOCI and FVTPL. In terms of FVOCI, FV changes are recorded in the OCI as part of the equity. Further, this FVOCI for debt instruments includes recycling, consequently a derecognition before maturity results in the transfer of the amount booked in the OCI into the P & L. In contrast to that, an equity instrument is permitted to opt in for the FVOCI at initial recognition as long as it is not held for trading (IFRS 9.5.7.5). The accounting approach is different to the FVOCI of the debt instrument as the FVOCI of an equity instrument is designated and not mandatory. Therefore, changes of the FV are recorded in the OCI but the amount is rather transferred to another equity position instead of recycling at derecognition (IFRS 9.B5.7.1) (PricewaterhouseCoopers Aktiengesellschaft Wirtschaftsprüfungsgesellschaft 2017a, 1122f.; Wagenhofer 2018, 510 and 515 and 578).

Classification	AC	FVOCI (designated)	FVOCI (mandatory)	FVTPL
Initial recognition	FV + transaction costs			FV
Measurement	AC	FV	FV	FV
Disagio/Agio etc.	P & L	Not used for equity instruments (IAS 32)	P & L	P & L
Change in FV	No consideration	OCI	OCI	P & L
Consideration of the Expected Loss	P & L	OCI	P & L	P & L

Table 1 | Measurement of financial assets

(Source: PricewaterhouseCoopers Aktiengesellschaft Wirtschaftsprüfungs-gesellschaft 2017a, 1124)

As shown in table one, there are four classification categories and each category is briefly summarised in regard to the initial recognition, measurement, disagio/agio, change in the FV and the consideration of the expected loss. In terms of the measurement, the main points are divided into AC and FV. Beginning with financial assets classified at AC, the measurement at AC requires the effective interest method according to IFRS 9.5.2.1. in connection with IFRS 9.4.2.1. As the difference of the face value and amount to be repaid is recorded in the interest income, the effective interest method is also relevant for FVOCI (mandatory) (PricewaterhouseCoopers Aktiengesellschaft Wirtschaftsprüfungs-gesellschaft 2017a, 1124; Wagenhofer 2018, 508ff.).

With reference to the measurement at AC, its definition also considers the expected loss. In fact, changes in value regarding derecognition, reclassification, expected loss or disagio/agio using the effective interest method are recorded in the P & L as stated in IFRS 9.5.7.2. In terms of the effective interest rate method, the aim is to determine the interest rate based on the difference of the face value and the amount repaid. As a result, the interest rate calculated is applied to evaluate the initial face value discounting interest and capital payments. The effective interest method includes loan origination fees and loan commitment fees (IFRS 9.B5.4.2), whereas IFRS 9.B5.4.3 list those components which are not allowed to consider such as loan administration fees, loan commitment fees if the loan agreement is unlikely to be closed and accrued-interest (PricewaterhouseCoopers Aktiengesellschaft Wirtschafts-prüfungsgesellschaft 2017a, 1125f.; Wagenhofer 2018, 515 and 567f.).

Neither IAS 39 nor IFRS 9 set a calculation approach to determine the effective interest rate. Nevertheless, the ISMA-approach (International Securities Market Association), Actual/Actual, 365/365 or Actual/365 approach as interest rates are also set for less than a year, are common ways. However, amortisation is set in IFRS 9.B5.4.4 under the condition that the duration of the financial asset is contractually stipulated. Further, it may even be amortised within a shorter period. For the calculation of the AC, the cash method is applied. Thus, the sum of all future cash flows is discounted by the effective interest rate considering the time component and where required the subtraction of the accrued interest. This procedure applies to floating-rate instruments at the interest rate fixing. In regard to disagio/agio, the market rate influences amortisation at the end of the next interest rate fixing. Further, changes in the creditworthiness impact amortisation at maturity. Moreover, contractual modifications and adaptions of the estimation are recorded in the P & L if the gross book value changes (PricewaterhouseCoopers Aktiengesellschaft Wirtschaftsprüfungsgesellschaft 2017a, 590 and 1126ff.; Wagenhofer 2018, 568).

In terms of the measurement at FV, the categories FVOCI (mandatory), FVTPL and FVOCI (designated) are described in the next paragraphs. First of all, changes in the FV are recorded in the P & L if the financial instrument belongs to the classification category FVTPL. However, it may occur that FV changes of held for trading instruments are recorded in the trading results, whereas instruments categorised as FVO are booked into the net results unless it is assigned to a portfolio measured at FV. Furthermore, foreign currency translation for financial assets measured at FVTPL are booked into the P & L. Compared to FVTPL, the FVOCI does not affect the P & L but the OCI. Referring to the FVOCI (mandatory), interest-bearing financial instruments are recorded under the position interest income in the P & L. Under the condition that a financial asset measured at FVOCI (mandatory) is derecognised, the FV changes are transferred from the OCI as part of the equity, into the P & L in accordance with IFRS 9.5.7.10. In regard to foreign currency translation, monetary financial instruments such as interest-bearing securities categorised at FVOCI (mandatory) are required to be separated into currency translation effects and FV changes. As stated in IFRS 9.B5.7.2A those changes occurred by currency translation are recorded in the P & L. While FVOCI (mandatory) includes recycling, FVOCI (designated) is not intended for recycling (IFRS 9.5.7.5). Nevertheless, dividends payable is recorded in the P & L (IFRS 9.5.7.6). Equity instruments for which the FVOCI option is chosen, foreign currency translation affect non-monetary financial instruments resulting in the recording of foreign currency changes in the OCI (IFRS 9.B5.7.3) (PricewaterhouseCoopers Aktiengesellschaft Wirtschaftsprüfungsgesellschaft 2017a, 1130ff.; Wagenhofer 2018, 515f. and 579).

While IAS 39 applied initial costs for non-equity instruments in case the determination of the FV is impossible, IFRS 9 set the FV as the only approach enabling measurement at initial costs for solely rare circumstances. This occurs mainly if too little information is available (IFRS 9.B5.2.3). Furthermore, the usage of initial costs is not allowed for banks and investment funds (PricewaterhouseCoopers Aktiengesellschaft Wirtschaftsprüfungsgesellschaft 2017a, 1132f.; Wagenhofer 2018, 567).

3.3.2 Financial Liabilities

In regard to the initial recognition, the approach for financial liabilities is equal to financial assets in accordance with IFRS 9.3.1.1 requiring recognition as it becomes part of a contract. Besides the legal obligation and the right evolving from a contract, also a firm commitment is recognised. However, future business transactions independent of its probability of occurrence are neither considered for financial assets nor liabilities (PricewaterhouseCoopers Aktiengesellschaft Wirtschaftsprüfungsgesellschaft 2017a, 1037; Wagenhofer 2018, 502f. and 535).

Regarding the derecognition of financial liabilities, IFRS 9 took over the standards from IAS 39. While the decision to derecognise financial assets is more demanding, the derecognition of financial liabilities respectively a part of the financial liability, is carried out at repayment, cancellation or expiration of the contract. In accordance with IFRS 9.B3.3.1 the derecognition is recognised if the financial liability is repaid based on the contractual agreement or if the debtor is legally released from the commitment. However, there are two exceptions where the legal release is not counted. As in IFRS 9.B3.3.4, the recognition of the financial liability is insofar mandatory as the debtor stipulated to pay to a third party. The second exception as stated in IFRS 9.B3.3.7 is the agreement of the debtor to an indemnity bond which indeed leads to a derecognition and a recognition of the new commitment (PricewaterhouseCoopers Aktiengesellschaft Wirtschaftsprüfungsgesellschaft 2017a, 1047f.; Wagenhofer 2018, 545).

Furthermore, a debt instrument bought back by the issuer also leads to derecognition. Nevertheless, this financial liability is not accounted as financial asset, therefore changes are recorded in the P & L independent from future sales. On the condition that the financial liability is repaid or the debtor is legally released (IFRS 9.B3.3.1), IFRS 9.3.3.3 prescribe for the derecognition that the difference between the carrying amount and the actual amount paid to be booked in the P & L (PricewaterhouseCoopers Aktiengesellschaft Wirtschafts-prüfungsgesellschaft 2017a, 1048; Wagenhofer 2018, 507 and 545).

Similarly to financial assets, financial liabilities are also derecognised if a modification leads to substantial changes. In accordance to IFRS 9.3.3.2 a repayment is considered as replacement of a financial instrument but also as modification of contract terms which influence the contractual cash flows. The financial liability is derecognised in order to recognise the financial liability with its modified characteristics. While for financial assets no explicitly defined range for significant changes exists, financial liabilities define a minimum change in the present value of 10 % to be substantial. Therefore, the present value is calculated prior to the modification and is afterwards compared to the result including the modification (PricewaterhouseCoopers Aktiengesellschaft Wirtschaftsprüfungsgesellschaft 2017a, 1049; Wagenhofer 2018, 507).

In terms of the definition of financial liabilities, IAS 32.11 refer generally to the presentation of financial instruments and considers a financial liability as the delivery of cash or other financial assets as well as the disadvantageous exchange of financial assets or liabilities to another company. Furthermore, liabilities are also contracts in own equity instruments unless it is a derivative instrument (PricewaterhouseCoopers Aktiengesellschaft Wirtschaftsprüfungs- gesellschaft 2017a, 1106; Wagenhofer 2018, 191f.).

Compared to financial assets, financial liabilities are still categorised as in IAS 39. Therefore, financial liabilities are either measured at AC or FVTPL. Regarding IFRS 9.4.2.1, financial liabilities are generally measured at AC unless the financial liability is listed under the exceptions. Thus, financial liabilities not measured at AC are financial liabilities measured at FVTPL, non-transferable financial assets which result in a financial liability but do not meet the requirements for derecognition, financial guarantees, promises for loans set at an interest below the market interest rate and conditional rewards in terms of mergers. In accordance with IFRS 9.4.4.2 a financial liability is prohibited for a reclassification once categorised (PricewaterhouseCoopers Aktiengesellschaft Wirtschaftsprüfungsgesellschaft 2017a, 1106f.; Wagenhofer 2018, 508ff.).

As stated in IFRS 9.4.2.1(a) which is the exception from the measurement at AC, it considers financial liabilities as well as derivatives with a negative market value for a measurement at FVTPL consequently affecting the P & L. In addition to that, it is vital to define financial liabilities intended for trading purposes. Therefore, IFRS 9.BA.6 describe trading as the regular buy and sale of financial assets aiming to generate profit from the volatility of prices. Nevertheless, IFRS 9.BA.8 set out that the measurement at FVTPL is not automatically conducted for financial liabilities held, thereby assuming held for trading. In fact, four financial liabilities meet the requirement in accordance with IFRS 9.BA.7. These financial liabilities are derivatives with a negative market value not intended as hedge instruments, the obligations delivering short sales, the short-term buyback of own debt instruments and those financial instruments categorised into a portfolio as long as there is evidence for the generation of profit in the recent past (PricewaterhouseCoopers Aktiengesellschaft Wirtschaftsprüfungs- gesellschaft 2017a, 1107f.; Wagenhofer 2018, 508 and 604).

However, even if the financial liability is not categorised as held for trading, it may be possible to irrevocably opt in for the FVO in case the requirements are met, enabling more relevant information. First of all, the FVO may be exercised if an accounting mismatch regarding the measurement of assets and liabilities respectively income and loss occurs in accordance with IFRS 9.4.2.2(a). As described in IFRS 9.B4.1.30(c), an accounting mismatch occurs if both financial asset and financial liability are exposed to the same risk and their FV changes move in an opposing trend. In order to reduce this accounting mismatch as those items offset each other, the FVO is applied. However, there is no obligation to obtain a financial asset or liability at the same time under the condition that every transaction is designated at the initial recognition (IFRS 9.B4.1.31). Secondly, the FVO is permitted for use if the risk management strategy aims for a portfolio of financial instruments or solely financial liabilities to be measured at FV and forwards the development to key positions within the company according to IFRS 9.4.2.2(b). Finally, hybrid contracts consisting of embedded derivatives and a host contract may also apply the FVO. The hybrid contract as total is permitted for designation under the condition that the host contract is a financial asset not affected by IFRS 9. Nevertheless, IFRS 9.4.3.5 list two exceptions which is the insignificance on contractual cash flows of the embedded derivatives on the one hand and similarity to other hybrid instruments which obviously indicate that separation is prohibited on the other side. Regarding embedded derivatives, the main reason to opt in for the FVO is to reduce complexity as otherwise each embedded derivative needs to be analysed and categorised appropriately (IFRS 9.B4.3.9) (PricewaterhouseCoopers Aktiengesellschaft Wirtschaftsprüfungsgesellschaft 2017a, 1108f.; Wagenhofer 2018, 509f. and 561 and 565).

With respect to the measurement of financial liabilities, the procedure is conform to financial assets. Therefore, financial liabilities are measured at FV at initial recognition including transaction costs in accordance with IFRS 9.5.1.1 (PricewaterhouseCoopers Aktiengesellschaft Wirtschaftsprüfungsgesellschaft 2017a, 1117; Wagenhofer 2018, 510).

Classification	FVTPL (designated)	FVTPL (held-for-trading)	AC
Initial recognition	FV	FV	FV + transaction costs
Measurement	FV	FV	AC
Disagio/Agio etc.	P & L	P & L	P & L
Change in FV due to the default risk	OCI unless accounting mismatch	P & L	No consideration
Other changes in FV	P & L	P & L	No consideration

Table 2 | Measurement of financial liabilities

(Source: PricewaterhouseCoopers Aktiengesellschaft Wirtschaftsprüfungs-gesellschaft 2017a, 1138)

As clearly presented in table two, the measurement of financial liabilities is categorised in FVTPL (designated), FVTPL (held-for-trading) and AC. Generally, financial liabilities are categorised and measured at AC according to IFRS 9.5.3.1 in connection with IFRS 9.4.2.1. As described in appendix A, AC of financial assets and financial liabilities result from the initial recognition for which amortisation is considered. For the amortisation, the difference between the initial amount and the amount paid at maturity for which the effective interest rate method is used, is calculated. However, IFRS 9.4.2.1. also define financial instruments not measured at AC. Consequently, financial liabilities categorised as FVTPL including those held-for-trading and for which the FVO is chosen and thus are FVTPL (designated), are measured at FV (IFRS 9.4.2.1(a)). Furthermore, if a financial asset is not transferable or it is a continuing involvement due to the authority to dispose resulting in a financial liability, the measurement follows IFRS 9.3.2.17 (IFRS 9.4.2.1(b)). As a result, the net book value is measured in accordance with the rights and obligations that remain with the financial asset and is either at AC or at FV. Moreover, financial guarantees for which IFRS 9.4.2.1(a)-(b) is not applicable, the higher amount of either the valuation adjustment of expected losses or the recorded amount of expected losses reduced by the amount which is already transferred to the P & L is used for measurement. An additional exception for the measurement at AC is commitments in regard to loans below the market interest rate unless measured at FVTPL, the procedure is the same as for financial guarantees. Finally, contingent considerations in terms of mergers are measured at FV (PricewaterhouseCoopers Aktiengesellschaft Wirtschaftsprüfungsgesellschaft 2017a, 1133ff.; Wagenhofer 2018, 506 and 508f. and 511 and 530).

As described in this chapter, the FVO and its measurement at FVTPL is allowed under the condition of an accounting mismatch or belonging to a group of financial instruments measured at FV in alliance with the risk management strategy (IFRS 9.4.2.2). In terms of derivatives, the measurement is conducted at FVTPL concerning derivatives with a negative market value, not assigned as hedge instrument and those embedded derivatives which allow for the separation of the derivative from the host contract remaining unchanged as in IAS 39. For financial commitments that contain at least one or more embedded derivative, the irrevocable designation as FVO is carried out unless the derivative impacts the contractual cash flows insignificantly or an invalid separation exists. As for financial assets, the FV for financial liabilities is equal to the transaction price in accordance with IFRS 9.B5.1.1 (PricewaterhouseCoopers Aktiengesellschaft Wirtschaftsprüfungsgesellschaft 2017a, 1135f.; Wagenhofer 2018, 509 and 566).

In terms of the FVO, the measurement requires the consideration of two risks measured separately. In accordance with IFRS 9.5.7.7 a financial instrument exercising the FVO and thus applying measurement at FV demands to separate the changes in the FV occurred through the default risk of the financial liability itself and the remaining changes of the FV. Due to that, the changes from the default risk are recorded in the OCI, whereas the part not traceable to the default risk is recorded in the P & L. Nevertheless, if this separation leads to an accounting mismatch, IFRS 9.5.7.8 permit to record both FV changes in the P & L. In fact, if the FVO is economically connected to a financial instrument and is also measured at FVTPL, then the changes in the default risk may be offset by the changes of the other instrument booked into the P & L. In addition, IFRS 9.B5.7.11 emphasise that there must be no contractual agreement between those two financial instruments but in order to switch from OCI to P & L, the financial liability needs to be adapted at the initial recognition (PricewaterhouseCoopers Aktiengesellschaft Wirtschaftsprüfungsgesellschaft 2017a, 1136ff.; Wagenhofer 2018, 515f. and 579f.).

In contrast to that, the measurement of loan commitments and financial guarantees at FV are independent from IFRS 9.5.7.7 recorded in the P & L (IFRS 9.5.7.9). With reference to the default risk, the definition in IFRS 9.B5.7.13 consider the risk of the issuer not meeting its obligations in regard to the financial liability. Thus, it does not focus on the creditworthiness of the issuer itself as the issuance of a secured liability leads to less risk than the issuance of an unsecured liability. The main hurdle to overcome in terms of FVO is the determination of FV changes resulting from the default risk. As stated in IFRS 9.B5.7.16, the evaluation of changes in the FV occurred through the default risk are those that are not traceable back to market risk changes or alternatively the development of an own method which enables to determine the default risk more precisely. In general, market risks result from changes in the reference rate, the price of another financial instrument within the company, the price of commodities, the exchange rate or the indices (IFRS 9.B5.7.17). With particular regard to transferring, changes in the FV resulting from the default risk recorded in the OCI are not transferrable to the P & L. Hence, the profit or loss recorded in the OCI is allowed to be transferred into the accumulated OCI. In terms of currency translation, financial assets and liabilities are recorded in the P & L in case of monetary positions according to IFRS 9.B5.7.2 (PricewaterhouseCoopers Aktiengesellschaft Wirtschaftsprüfungsgesellschaft 2017a, 1136ff.; Wagenhofer 2018, 515f. and 578ff. and 581).

4 Balance Sheet and Profit-and-Loss Account

In this chapter the importance of the IFRS framework is described. Due to the fact that the IFRS framework requires a fair presentation of the financial statements, it is necessary to analyse the relevant financial statements in detail and determine key information which is inevitable in the decision-making process for current and potential investors. However, this approach implies that the going-concern principle is met. In terms of the financial statements, IFRS require to include the balance sheet, profit and loss statement, statement of other comprehensive income, statement of changes in equity, cash flow statement and appendix. This paper focuses on the balance sheet, profit-and-loss account including OCI and the asset and liability management (ALM), the financial accounting and the role of the risk management (Müller and Saile 2018, 57; Zülch and Hendler 2017, 58f. and 63).

4.1 Asset Liability Management

The ALM manages interest rate and liquidity risk on an aggregated level for business lines within the bank. Movements in the interest rate affect the value of assets and liabilities, whereas a mismatch between assets and liabilities and the allocation of additional funds is assigned to the liquidity management. According to Bohn and Tanucci there are four risk types to consider, the maturity transformation, behavioural risk, structural risk and the basis risk. All of them create an interest rate risk characterised by either short- or long-term maturities. In contrast to that, the refinancing risk only evolves from maturity transformation and behavioural risks. Regarding the task of ALM, it is to limit and manage the market risk in the balance sheet, meet regulations, such as Basel III, and further limiting internal guidelines. Moreover, ALM coordinates money market activities within the whole bank (Bohn and Tonucci 2014, 59f.; Choudhry 2007, 5 and 211f.; Enthofer and Haas 2016, 41).

Compared to ALM, financial accounting is responsible for preparing the financial statements relevant for investors. As a result, financial accounting analyses, records, summarises and reports economic events that occur within the company (Horngren et al. 2014, 5 and 7).

While the regulatory capital requirements are described in chapter 4.2. focusing on the risk management, it is advisable to consider the terms banking and trading book as it affects the P & L. In terms of the banking book, activities such as deposits and loans are covered and contain the traditional banking operations. The criterion which leads to the assignment into the banking book is the type of the business activity independent of the counterparty. For accounting, interest cash flows are recorded in accordance with the accruals principle. The assets and liabilities assigned to the banking book are an interest rate and credit risk exposure for the bank and generate liquidity and maturity transformation risk. While the aim of the banking book is to buy and hold assets for a longer period, the trading book's objective is the trading which leads to a minimum holding period of a day. As the trading book follows the activity of market making and proprietary trading, mark-to-market approach is applied. Thus, daily movements in the market value are recorded in the P & L as unrealised profit and loss. However, the actual profit respectively loss is compared to the initial mark at derecognition. Furthermore, the trading book contains derivatives e.g. futures and swaps which are not recorded in the balance sheet but rather off-balance as these derivatives are considered as future exposures not necessarily demanding a cash outflow or inflow. As with the banking book, the trading book creates the same risk exposure including market risk, credit risk and liquidity risk for the bank (Choudhry 2007, 7f.).

4.1.1 Individual consideration of the profit-and-loss account

The P & L is a report that illustrates revenues and expenses for a given time period and results either in a net income or a net loss. The main difference between the P & L and the balance sheet is the period. While the P & L presents the performance over a given period of time, the balance sheet is a snapshot in time. In terms of the banking sector, the revenues in the P & L are made up of the net interest income, fees and commissions as well as trading income. In order to achieve a profit, the expenses e.g. operating expenses, loan loss provisions, trading losses and tax expenses must be less than the revenues generated (Choudhry 2007, 12f.; Horngren et al. 2014, 58f.).

The basis for maintaining the going-concern principle is partially the achievement of a net interest income (NII) for a retail bank. Thus, a bank generates revenues if it provides loans and manages to earn a net yield that outweighs the cost of funding. Apart from lending, ALM also considers the entire investment portfolio of the bank which may include earnings in form of coupon or dividend payments. However, the cost of funding impacts the NII due to the fact that solely a few options are available, for instance deposits, capital markets, interbank money markets or covered bonds. Moreover, it is necessary to consider that high interest margins might also result in higher risk held by the bank. Additionally, the NII is exposed to the credit risk and market risk. In regard to the balance sheet, the aim is to match the maturity of an asset with its liability used for funding. Unless the maturity deviates, the bank profits from rising interest rates if the assets maturity is reached sooner. In contrast to that, if maturity transformation fails, the bank faces decreasing interest rates. Consequently, interest income is influenced by the interest rate and the maturity transformation. In case of a low interest phase, the bank is possibly exposed to a net interest loss, respectively a negative NII, if those additional costs are not charged for customers (Choudhry 2007, 13f.). Other revenues such as the fee and commission income is not directly exposed to market risk but is still not risk free. However, it is a relatively easy approach for generating revenues. In contrast, trading income is riskier but also involves higher returns. Nevertheless, a bank is responsible to hold provisions for unexpected losses. While provisions are deducted from the loan revenues if losses increase, it is also possible to transfer a percentage to the loan revenues. Finally, operating expenses evolve from human resources, infrastructure, depreciation and goodwill (Choudhry 2007, 14f. and 17).

In regard to the profit and loss statement and statement of other comprehensive income, the amendments also required changes in this area. Due to IFRS 9, additional positions including in the P & L are the

- result of other financial instruments mandatorily measured at FV,
- result from reclassifying financial assets measured at AC to FVTPL on the one hand and
- financial assets measured at FVOCI to FVTPL on the other hand,
- result from financial assets measured at AC,
- result from derecognised financial assets measured at FVOCI and
- result from derecognised financial assets measured at AC (PricewaterhouseCoopers Aktiengesellschaft Wirtschaftsprüfungsgesellschaft 2017a, 418ff. and 421ff.).

This implies that the positions which reflect the categorisation under IAS 39 (i.e. AFS, HTM and L&R) are replaced. Moreover, the additional position required to be transferred into the P & L is the change in the reserves resulting from financial assets measured at FVOCI. However, there are also additional positions which are not supposed for a transfer into the P & L, for instance the change in the reserve from equity instruments measured at FVOCI and the change in the reserve arising from the own credit risk (PricewaterhouseCoopers Aktiengesellschaft Wirtschaftsprüfungsgesellschaft 2017a, 418ff. and 421ff.).

4.1.2 Overall view of the balance sheet

The balance sheet is the presentation of the assets and liabilities. While the assets show the application of funds, the liabilities illustrate the source of funds as debt and equity of the bank. Generally, a balance sheet of a bank is similar to one of a company. However, the main difference is the business model due to the fact that the bank provides e.g. loans to private customers or companies. As a result, the balance sheet contains loans provided to households and firms and other assets such as liquid assets held on the asset side, whereas the liability side includes the funding through households and firms current accounts, wholesale funding and its capital (Farag, Harland and Nixon 2014, 26ff. and 48; Zülch and Hendler 2017, 106).

Assets (IAS 39)	Liabilities (IAS 39)
Loan claims	Liabilities due to banks
Customer claims	Liabilities due to customers
Assets held for dealing purposes	Liabilities from dealing activities
FV designated financial assets	FV designated financial liabilities
Hedge instruments	Hedge instruments
AFS assets	
HTM assets	

Table 3 | Balance Sheet under IAS 39

(Source: PricewaterhouseCoopers Aktiengesellschaft Wirtschaftsprüfungs-gesellschaft 2017a, 405)

Assets (IFRS 9)	Liabilities (IFRS 9)
Loan claims	Liabilities due to banks
Customer claims	Liabilities due to customers
Assets held for dealing purposes	Liabilities from dealing activities
FV designated (other) financial assets (mandatory)	FV designated financial liabilities
FV designated financial assets	Hedge instruments
Hedge instruments	
FVOCI financial assets	
FVOCI equity instruments	
AC financial assets	

Table 4 | Balance Sheet under IFRS 9

(Source: PricewaterhouseCoopers Aktiengesellschaft Wirtschaftsprüfungs-gesellschaft 2017a, 406f.)

Comparing table three and table four, the changes in IFRS 9 result in the reorganisation of the items in the balance sheet which is briefly illustrated. As observable in the tables, IFRS 9 include more items on the asset side due to the classification categories (PricewaterhouseCoopers Aktiengesellschaft Wirtschaftsprüfungsgesellschaft 2017a, 1138).

As long as an IFRS 9 balance sheet focuses on the liability side, there are further items listed such as equity, provisions, liabilities as well as accruals and deferred items. From a standard balance sheet point of view, the equity is divided into sub-items e.g. subscribed capital, capital reserves and retained earnings. Due to the emphasis on the OCI in this paper, the equity also consists of the sub-items reserves for financial assets measured at FVOCI, reserves for equity instruments measured at FVOCI and reserves from the measurement of the own credit spread. These specific sub-items are not included in a balance sheet applying IAS 39. While the balance sheet has a yearly rolling basis, the P & L is set up for a specific period and profits are added to or losses are written off on the balance sheet at the closing date (Heesen 2017, 4f. and 12; PricewaterhouseCoopers Aktiengesellschaft Wirtschaftsprüfungsgesellschaft 2017a, 416f.).

4.2 Risk Management

In terms of risk, due to the large number of existing definitions, a common understanding when speaking about risk management is of crucial importance. While there are similarities between the risk management of a bank and of a company, the risks in a bank affect the deposits of privates and institutions, thereby the financial system and its stability. In order to protect the savings, banks are demanded to comply with specific regulations set by the supervising central bank (Población García 2017, 4 and 14).

Such regulations belong to the macroprudential policy, which aims at reducing and avoiding systemic risk which affects the whole financial system. Idiosyncratic risk on the other side only affects individual institutions. As a result, various requirements have been introduced, such as the regulatory minimum requirement in regard to the loan-to-value ratio, which aims to prevent excessive lending to customers and consequently, the occurrence of a financial crisis. The capital regulation is of high relevance in the banking sector for which the responsible body is the Basel Committee on Banking Supervision (BCBS) which belongs to the Bank for International Settlements (BIS). The current Basel III has been adapted based on the previously applied Basel I and Basel II. The objective respectively the focus of Basel III includes various topics. First of all, it focuses on the risks on and off the balance sheet and exposures resulting from derivatives. Secondly, it affects regulatory requirements for Counterparty Credit Risk, over the counter (OTC) as well as Securities Financing Transactions. Moreover, Basel III essentially deals with the amount and quality of capital and also aims at enhancing the funding and the liquidity of banks (Kemp 2017, 24f. and 117; Koulafetis 2017, 39).

In terms of the requirement of Basel III, it can be distinguished between three pillars: minimum capital requirements in pillar one, supervisory review process in pillar two and market discipline in pillar three. To begin with, pillar one defines the minimum capital requirements for a banks market risk, credit risk and operational risk. With Basel III, the total regulatory capital requirement amounts to 10.5 % which includes the Common Equity Tier 1 Capital (4.5 %), the capital conservation buffer (2.5 %), the additional Tier 1 capital (1.5 %) and the Tier 2 capital (2 %). Furthermore, a buffer for systemic risk and systemically important institutions (SIIs) as well as a countercyclical capital buffer is applied by the regulators increasing the total regulatory capital requirement by 7.5 % amounting to a total of 18 %. Pillar two focuses on the Internal Capital Adequacy Assessment Process (ICAAP), which ensures the maintenance of capital to cover risks within the bank, and the Supervisory Review and Evaluation Process (SREP) that examines capital, liquidity and risk management procedures of the bank. Finally, pillar three deals with the market discipline enhancements and requires the procedure on the calculation of the regulatory capital ratios. In order to implement Basel III, the European Union developed the Capital Requirements Directive (CRD) IV. In general, a directive aims to provide instructions while a regulation is mandatory and applicable for banks located in the European Union. Therefore, the CRR mainly contains prudential requirements for credit institutions and investment companies. Compared to the CRR, the CRD intends to focus on transparency regarding the activities of banks and investment funds but also the profit and loss (Koulafetis 2017, 208ff. and 211; Tian 2017, 6ff.)

5 Banking products on the liability side and annual statement analysis

Based on the theoretical input in chapter three that deals with IFRS 9 in regard to the valuation, classification and measurement of financial assets and liabilities and chapter four that describes the balance sheet, P & L and risk management, this chapter sets the focus on financial liabilities. As described in the objective of the examination, two points are examined. First of all, the necessity to opt in for the FVO is illustrated by the usage of three banking products on the liability side: deposits from customers, deposits from banks and own issuances. The terms and conditions, influencing and impact factors as well as the measurement of the three financial liabilities is described. Secondly, the banking products are compared with the annual statement analysis in order to determine whether deviations in the treatment are observable. Before the banking products are listed, it is advisable to consider the tasks and the specification of banks. Generally, a bank grants loans and accepts deposits. Therefore, the topic in this chapter is set on deposits from customers as well as deposits from banks. In terms of the specification of the banking, banks are categorised into retail banking, wholesale banking, universal banking and international banking. As a matter of fact, the separation is complicated as banks operate in more areas than deposits and loans. For instance, a bank might offer investment banking, asset management and other services provided to private customers, companies or institutions. While banks operate in more areas and thereby fulfil the requirements of a universal bank, there are still banks that focus solely on retail banking whereas other banks mainly specify in wholesale banking services (Matthews and Thompson 2008, 51f.). Apart from the comparison of the balance sheet applying IAS 39 and IFRS 9 in the previous chapter, the following illustration provides an overview of a hypothetical bank in regard to its balance sheet (Matthews and Thompson 2008, 150):

Assets		Liabilities	
Cash	50	Deposits from customers	500
Liquid assets	250	Deposits from banks	320
Loans and advances	700	Bonds	200
Fixed assets	100	Equity	80
Total assets	1100	Total liabilities	1100

Table 5 | Balance Sheet of a hypothetical bank

(Source: Matthews and Thompson 2008, 150)

5.1 Deposits from customers

In order to show whether the measurement of deposits in terms of IAS 39 or IFRS 9 respectively changed, it is essential to define the term deposits. There are three types of deposits that can be categorised under the term deposits from customers. First of all, sight deposits that mature daily are usually distinguished between deposits from banks and non-banks. However, as the next chapter emphasises deposits from banks, the sight deposit focuses on non-banks. Sight deposits are available to be withdrawn from the current account evolving from the credit balance. Although sight deposits are available unconditionally for withdrawal thus justifying the relatively little interest, the bank still uses deposits that result from the deposit base. Secondly, time deposits are in contrast to sight deposits characterised by the time limitation since these deposits commonly require a minimum amount for investment e.g. EUR 5,000. Furthermore, time deposits are interest-bearing investments for firms but also for banks to reallocate additional liquid resources. Finally, the third type of deposit is the savings deposit which is suitable for many individuals as an easy approach of investing. In comparison to time deposits, savings deposits enable to invest lower amounts (Hartmann-Wendels, Pfingsten and Weber 2015, 211 and 213ff.).

5.1.1 Terms and conditions

With respect to the terms and conditions of deposits from customers there are a few aspects to consider. As a bank, deposits from customers are categorised as debt and require the payment of interest and repayment of capital to the customers. In case the bank becomes insolvent, the debtors e.g. the customers are entitled to receive the payments, thereby putting shareholders on the second rank. Further, deposits are usually of short-term availability for the bank. Nevertheless, money must not be taken away from the account by customers but rather give the possibility to withdraw at any time. Consequently, deposits from customers are not intended for trading which leads to less flexibility for a bank. Finally, customers may decide to withdraw money from the account for investments. If there is no bank run which results in more customers to withdraw money, the bank is able to return the deposits. Assuming from a customer's point of view that a bank's creditworthiness deteriorates, the majority of customers withdraws their money, resulting in the outflow of liquidity. Consequently, a bank faces liquidity problem as deposits are used to fund loans (Hartmann-Wendels, Pfingsten and Weber 2015, 218f.).

The management of deposits from customers is linked to the funds management which aims to set volume, mix, return and cost of not only the liability side but also considers the reciprocation on the asset side. Consequently, the management of the asset side needs to be in line with liabilities in order to generate profit – from loans on the asset side and the management of the liabilities – and control costs and risks. Nevertheless, the liquidity management is responsible for the funding sources. The crucial point for deposits is the price affected by interest rates and other additionally offered terms. In regard to the interest rate, the supply of and demand for loanable funds cannot guarantee an interest rate but is rather based on current trends and other external factors. Thus, volatile situations occur (Rose and Hudgins 2013, 218ff.).

5.1.2 Influencing factors and impact factors

As discussed in chapter four, ALM is responsible for managing risks occurring in the balance sheet. In terms of deposits, there are a few risks that influence and impact the outcome. One of those risks evolves from the maturity transformation. The maturity transformation is the task of combining short- and long-term maturities on the asset and liability sides. Moreover, the rollover approach aims to refinance for instance loans on the asset side by short-term debt on the liability side. Due to that, liquidity risk arises. Consequently, if deposits are withdrawn from accounts, liquidity resources of the bank may be affected. Indeed, the maturity transformation may lead to bank runs unless a deposit guarantee scheme is set up by either the bank itself or the government. As a result, individuals are assured that deposits are repaid. Furthermore, the maturity transformation leads to interest rate risk as interest rates for short and long-term maturities differentiate. While the common case is that the interest rate for long-terms exceeds the interest rate of short-terms enabling the bank to profit from this spread, it also occurs that short-term interest rates are higher than those of long-terms resulting in a negative spread (Bessis 2010, 29f.; Hartmann-Wendels, Pfingsten and Weber 2015, 218 and 233; Matthews and Thompson 2008, 54).

As deposits from customers are a vital component of a bank, the costs resulting from deposits are relevant for the pricing. The bank aims to obtain new funds and generate profit on the one side but also faces the problem of passing on the costs to customers and determining the interest rate neither losing business nor profit on the other side. As a result, a bank might apply the cost-plus pricing formula which delivers the unit price for each deposit service for a customer as the sum of the operating expense per unit of the deposit service, the estimated overhead expenses that refer to the deposit service and the planned profit margin from each service unit sold. In contrast to that, the interest rate set on deposits can also be determined by the marginal cost which is the cost of additional funds. This approach is forward-looking and does not rely on the average cost from the past, which enables a bank to adapt marginal costs if interest rates fluctuate. In order to determine to which extent the interest rate is determined and at which point it breaks even, in other words the additional cost of deposits leads to no profit or to a decreasing profit, two parameters are required. First of all, the marginal cost is the difference between the multiplication of the new interest rate and total funds raised at this new rate and the multiplication of the old interest rate and total funds raised at this old rate. Secondly, the relation between the change in total cost and the additional funds raised result in the marginal cost rate which is used as comparison to the marginal revenue resulting from the new deposits. The third approach to determine the costs for a deposit is the conditional pricing. The concept of this pricing method is to charge fees under the condition of the deposit balance. Hence, if the average balance falls below a predetermined minimum, the customer is obliged to pay higher fees, while keeping it above the minimum leads to no or low fee payment of the customer. Nevertheless, it is recommendable to consider components such as the frequency of transactions, the defined average balance of the deposit as well as the maturity (Rose and Hudgins 2013, 407 and 409ff.).

5.1.3 Measurement

The measurement of deposits from customers is shown by an example that aims to illustrate the theoretical input from IAS 39 and IFRS 9 and evaluates possible differences and variations from the measurement at AC, FVTPL and the right to exercise the FVO (PricewaterhouseCoopers Aktiengesellschaft Wirtschaftsprüfungsgesellschaft 2017a, 559). Due to the fact, that deposits from customers are considered for materiality, the fair presentation is achieved by separating them from deposits from banks. In accordance with IAS 32.11 it is necessary to distinguish between a liability and equity. Therefore, the repayment of capital and interest on deposits is treated as a liability. Moreover, the term customer needs to be defined. As IFRS list no explicit definition, the bank is requested to define or classify respectively the item and similar items in line with the business objective as prescribed in IAS 8.10f. and IAS 1.58. Once those items are indicated, it is mandatory to apply this approach consistently in the balance sheet and is requested to be disclosed in the appendix (IAS 1.45 and IAS 1.15) (PricewaterhouseCoopers Aktiengesellschaft Wirtschafts-prüfungsgesellschaft 2017b, 1928f.; Wagenhofer 2018, 28 and 32ff. and 65 and 191f.).

The objective of the measurement is to summarise the procedure using first IAS 39 and secondly IFRS 9 for deposits from customers. The main points discussed are the initial recognition, the classification and measurement and the consideration of the FVO. Moreover, the effect is shown using a sample calculation. Due to the fact that the standards IAS 39.10 to IAS 39.70 are repealed, the single standards used in this chapter are taken from PricewaterhouseCoopers Aktiengesellschaft Wirtschaftsprüfungsgesellschaft 2017a. To begin with, IAS 39.14 prescribe for financial instruments i.e. deposits for customers, to be part of a contract for the initial recognition. In regard to the classification, a financial liability is either classified at FVTPL or at AC under the condition that the financial instrument is defined as a liability, for instance due to the contractual obligation which requests to transfer cash or financial instruments (PricewaterhouseCoopers Aktiengesellschaft Wirtschaftsprüfungs-gesellschaft 2017a, 532 and 559; Wagenhofer 2018, 300).

In terms of the FVTPL category, IAS 39 includes two sub-categories: those financial liabilities held-for-trading as well as financial liabilities opting for the FVO. Due to the fact that deposits from customers are withdrawn, deposits are not intended as held-for-trading. Instead held-for-trading items are obligations that result from short selling or liabilities that occur as part of financial instruments held-for-trading. Compared to that, the irrevocable decision to opt in for the FVO is based on few requirements. Generally, IAS 39.9(b) set the objective for the use of the FVO that states the improvement of the presentation of the financial statements, leading to less complexity than the measurement at AC due to an accounting mismatch or the portfolio of financial instruments is measured at FV according to the business strategy. Under the condition that the requirement to opt in for the FVO is fulfilled, FV changes are booked into the P & L. As with IAS 39, also those FV changes resulting from the own creditworthiness are recorded in the P & L. Consequently, if the financial liability of a bank is measured at FVTPL and the creditworthiness deteriorates leading to a decrease in the FV, the improvement of this FV is considered as profit although the bank is worse off. In order to show a fair presentation of financial results, IFRS 7.10(a) state that changes in the own creditworthiness are requested to be described in the appendix. Nevertheless, the profit booked into the P & L from this decrease is transferred into equity which leads to an increase in equity. However, owing to the CRR, FV changes resulting from the own default risk that are transferred into equity are not allowed for prudential capital resource. However, in regard to deposits from customers, IAS 39 categorise such liabilities at AC which is also commonly used in practice (PricewaterhouseCoopers Aktiengesellschaft Wirtschaftsprüfungsgesellschaft 2017a, 539f. and 559f.).

With regards to the measurement at AC, deposits are recorded at the FV including transaction costs (IAS 39.43), which equal the historical acquisition cost. Due to the fact that financial assets such as HTM and L&R are identically measured as financial liabilities at AC, the following example is taken from PricewaterhouseCoopers Aktiengesellschaft Wirtschaftsprüfungsgesellschaft 2017a. Prior to the illustration of the example, the measurement at AC is conducted by applying the effective interest rate method. The aim is to determine the interest rate which evolves from the difference between the amount paid and the amount repayable. As a result, future interest and capital payments are discounted to the amount repayable including costs such as the loan origination or loan commitment fees but also disagios/agios. The formula using the Act/365 method is as follows (PricewaterhouseCoopers Aktiengesellschaft Wirtschaftsprüfungsgesellschaft 2017a, 577 and 587ff.):

$$AKt_0 = \sum_{i=1}^{n} \frac{CFt_i}{\left(1 + r_{eff}\right)^{\frac{t_i - t_0}{365}}}$$

Equation 1 | Act/365

AKt$_0$	Acquisition cost at t$_0$
CFt$_i$	Cash flows including interest and capital payment
t$_i$	Time of the CFt$_i$ payment
t$_0$	Valuation date
n	Maturity/Interest rate adjustment date
r$_{eff}$	Effective interest rate

Table 6 | Abbreviation for the Act/365 Method

(Source: PricewaterhouseCoopers Aktiengesellschaft Wirtschaftsprüfungs-gesellschaft 2017a, 589)

Example – Deposits from customers measured at AC (using the effective interest rate method)

01.01.2001: Bank buys a bond, principal is 100,000 and nominal interest is 10 %, maturity of five years, disagio on the date of purchase is 5 %

Cash flows:

01.01.01	31.12.01	31.12.02	31.12.03	31.12.04	31.12.05
-95,000	+10,000	+10,000	+10,000	+10,000	+110,000

As described, the effective interest rate is iteratively calculated – e.g. with Excel – by entering the amount payable at the beginning of the investment. The result of the effective interest rate is 11,3653 % which leads to a disagio due to the nominal interest of 10 % paid.

Thus, the disagio amounts in total to:

5 x 10,000 * 10 % = 5,000

Time	Interest income	Disagio	Balance sheet disclosure
t_1	10,797	797	95,797
t_2	10,888	888	96,685
t_3	10,989	989	97,674
t_4	11,100	1,100	98,774
t_5	11,226	1,226	100,000
Sum	55,000	5,000	-

Accounting entry at the initial recognition (01.01.01):

Bond   95,000

Interest expense (P & L) 5,000   /   Liabilities to banks   100,000

As a result, the disagio for the respective time is written off, e.g. for t_1, affecting the P & L:

Accrued items (disagio) / Interest expense (P & L)   797

Table 7 | Example – Deposits from customers measured at AC (using the effective interest rate method)

(Source: PricewaterhouseCoopers Aktiengesellschaft Wirtschaftsprüfungsgesellschaft 2017a, 589)

The AC is determined by substituting the value date by the balance sheet date in equation one, thereby the future cash flows are discounted with the effective interest rate. In case the financial instruments pay variable interest, the effective interest rate is adapted unless the book value of the financial instrument is close to the amount repayable at maturity. Otherwise the cash flows are required to be revalued in order to indicate interest income or interest loss, respectively. In terms of the example shown in table seven, a disagio exists at the time of contribution. According to IAS 39.AG6, the treatment of disagios/agios depends on two circumstances. On the one side, if the interest rate changes due to market conditions the amount is amortised until the next interest rate adjustment date. On the other side, if the interest rate changes are due to other market conditions or caused by changes in the own creditworthiness that are not manageable until the next interest rate adjustment date, the disagio/agio is amortised until the financial instruments matures. While disagio/agio are booked into the P & L, other changes only affect the P & L in case of the derecognition of a financial instrument (IAS 39.56). Moreover, the effective interest rate method which is used for financial liabilities measured at AC is relevant for the accrued interest. In addition, the right of the customer to cancel the contract is necessary to be reviewed due to the separation of an embedded derivative. At the recognition of a financial liability, the effective interest rate is applied by estimating the maturity, thereby considering the time of cancellation of the deposit. Consequently, the amount repayable at recognition equals the AC. The separation of the right of cancellation is requested unless the effective interest rate is determined in the way that the AC equal the amount repayable regardless of the time of cancellation (PricewaterhouseCoopers Aktiengesellschaft Wirtschaftsprüfungsgesellschaft 2017a, 590ff. and 652; PricewaterhouseCoopers Aktiengesellschaft Wirtschafts-prüfungsgesellschaft 2017b, 1930f.).

Apart from the measurement at AC, deposits from customers may be measured at FVTPL, opting for the FVO. The amount recorded is the FV excluding the transaction costs. While the measurement at AC generally only considers disagio/agio to be booked into the P & L, every change in the FV using the measurement at FVTPL is booked into the P & L. Assuming that a bank owns a portfolio of commercial papers categorised as AFS, derivatives categorised as held-for-trading and deposits from customers measured at AC, the risk management of the bank may decide to compromise these items as one portfolio measured at FV. As a result, each item is reclassified into FVTPL based on the objective of the risk management. Apart from that, commercial papers do not affect the P & L but are booked instead into the OCI, while held-for-trading affects P & L and deposits from customers are measured at AC (PricewaterhouseCoopers Aktiengesellschaft Wirtschaftsprüfungsgesellschaft 2017a, 545 and 577).

In line with the FV measurement IAS 39 refer to IFRS 13 which are relevant in regard to the assessment of financial liabilities and own equity instruments. The definition of the FV is explained by the fictional transfer which is the price paid by the debtor in order to transfer the financial liability and the willingness of the fictional company to take this financial liability according to IFRS 13.34. This approach is applicable for deposits from customers as the treatment reflects an original liability. In terms of how the FV is assessed, IFRS 13.35ff. lists a ranking regarding the method used. The first step is to determine an exit price if it exists in the market. Thus, market participants must buy and sell liabilities and equity instruments. Due to few market participants in this area, the second and in this case final step is to evaluate if there are corresponding financial assets. As a liability is most likely part of a financial asset, deposits from customers are evaluated based on IFRS 13.37 which lead to a FV that is equal to the corresponding financial assets' amount. However, there might be the need to adapt the FV due to factors influencing solely the asset side. If provided, financial assets are measured at FV using the market price. Nevertheless, for the financial liability a revaluation is requested as bid-ask spreads or selling restrictions decrease the FV of the financial asset. It is important to point out, however, that the FV of demand deposits must exceed or equal the amount repayable, thereby indicating that the calculation of the effective interest rate method is still of relevance due to the period of notice (PricewaterhouseCoopers Aktiengesellschaft Wirtschaftsprüfungsgesellschaft 2017a, 638 and 1251ff.). In terms of deposits from customers measured at FVTPL, the example shown in table seven is adapted using two scenarios (PricewaterhouseCoopers Aktiengesellschaft Wirtschaftsprüfungsgesellschaft 2017a, 589):

Example – Deposits from customers measured at FVTPL (IAS 39)

01.01.2001: Bank owns deposits from customers amounting to a FV of 100,000 assuming there is no right of cancellation

- Scenario 1: Due to the FV change of the corresponding financial asset, the current FV of the deposits amounts to 90,000 (own creditworthiness remains unchanged)
- Scenario 2: The rating agency Moody's decreases the rating of the bank from Aaa to Aa2 leading to a decrease in the FV of the deposits totalling to 85,000

The two scenarios refer to those FV changes which are not considered when measuring the financial liability at AC. While agios and disagios are booked into the P & L, the main focus in this example is set on the two other FV changes.

Scenario 1: The FV decreases by 10,000 thus affecting the P & L

Gains FVTPL (P & L) / Deposits from customers   10,000

Scenario 2: The FV decreases by 15,000 caused by the own creditworthiness, affecting the P & L and require to be included in the appendix

Gains FVTPL (P & L) / Deposits from customers   15,000

Table 8 | Example - Deposits from customers measured at FVTPL (IAS 39)

(Source: PricewaterhouseCoopers Aktiengesellschaft Wirtschaftsprüfungs-gesellschaft 2017a, 589)

Based on the two examples illustrated, the main difference between the measurement of deposits at AC or FVTPL, is the consideration of changes in the P & L. Using the FVTPL, all changes that affect the FV are recorded in the P & L and afterwards are booked against the equity when the annual accounts are drawn up. In contrast, the measurement at AC affects only the P & L in case of disagios/agios (PricewaterhouseCoopers Aktiengesellschaft Wirtschafts-prüfungsgesellschaft 2017a, 640f.).

In terms of the derecognition, a financial liability is only allowed for derecognition if it is written-off, in other words the liability is settled or legally released, cancelled or expired (IAS 39.39) (PricewaterhouseCoopers Aktiengesellschaft Wirtschaftsprüfungsgesellschaft 2017a, 714). In regard to IFRS 9, the initial recognition is conform to IAS 39 prescribing for a contractual agreement. In addition, the derecognition of financial liabilities is equal to IAS 39 (PricewaterhouseCoopers Aktiengesellschaft Wirtschaftsprüfungsgesellschaft 2017a, 1037 and 1047).

Further, IFRS 9 is applied as stated in IAS 39 apart from the fact that the standards are listed in the section of IFRS 9. Consequently, the two classification categories: at AC and FVTPL including held-for-trading and the FVO are unchanged. Moreover, as in IAS 39 financial liabilities are not allowed for reclassification (PricewaterhouseCoopers Aktiengesellschaft Wirtschafts-prüfungsgesellschaft 2017a, 1106ff. and 1109).

While the measurement of financial liabilities at AC is unchanged, the example in table seven using the effective interest rate method is conform with the measurement in IFRS 9. In contrast, the measurement at FVTPL regarding the FVO changed and thereby the treatment is adapted in terms of FV changes due to changes in the credit risk. While those changes are booked into the P & L and are included in the appendix in IAS 39, IFRS 9 splits FV changes booked into the P & L from FV changes owing to the default risk which is transferred into the OCI (PricewaterhouseCoopers Aktiengesellschaft Wirtschaftsprüfungs-gesellschaft 2017a, 1124 and 1133 and 1136).

In order to show the difference between deposits measured at FVTPL using IAS 39 and IFRS 9, the example illustrated in table seven is modified. Additionally, it is assumed that the FV changes due to the credit spread do not cause an accounting mismatch (PricewaterhouseCoopers Aktiengesellschaft Wirtschaftsprüfungsgesellschaft 2017a, 589):

Example – Deposits from customers measured at FVTPL (IFRS 9)
01.01.2001: Bank owns deposits from customers amounting to a FV of 100,000
Due to interest rate changes, the FV of the corresponding financial asset changes and leads the current FV of the deposits to decrease. In addition, the rating agency Moody's decreases the rating of the bank from Aaa to Aa2 leading to a decrease in the FV of the deposits. The current value of the deposits from customers amounts to 85,000 assuming one third is traceable back to the interest rate while the remaining part is due to default risk of the bank.
FV change resulting from the interest rate booked into the P & L: Interest income FVO (P & L) / Deposits from customers   5,000
FV change due to the decrease of the FV (1) but increase of the default risk of the bank (2): (1) Deposits from customers / Gain FVTPL (P & L)   10,000 (2) Gain FVTPL / Accumulated OCI   10,000

Table 9 | Example – Deposits from customers measured at FVTPL (IFRS 9)

(Source: PricewaterhouseCoopers Aktiengesellschaft Wirtschaftsprüfungs-gesellschaft 2017a, 589)

As shown in table nine, the OCI is used for the default risk whereas all other changes affect the P & L. Moreover, assuming deposits meet the requirements for derecognition, the amounts booked into the OCI are not transferred into the P & L but rather into equity e.g. accumulated OCI. Consequently, OCI is not intended for recycling. Finally, the measurement at AC remains unchanged applying either IAS 39 or IFRS 9. As a result, disagio/agio – for instance interest expenses – are the only items that are booked into the P & L. Other than that, the measurement at FVTPL and the decision to opt in for the FVO leads to a different treatment. The application of IAS 39 lead to the recording of FV changes of the financial liability e.g. the deposit from customer in the P & L. The closing of the P & L affects the equity as that the outweigh of the gains over the expenses lead to a net income and an increase in equity. The opposite, which means that expenses exceed the gains, lead to a decrease in equity. FV changes are recorded in the P & L as with IAS 39 but FV changes traceable back to the default risk are shown in the balance sheet under the accumulated OCI as part of the equity. Thereby, FV changes are recorded in the P & L whereas changes from the default risk are booked against the OCI which directly affects equity. The decision to exercise the FVO is more relevant for IFRS 9 as IAS 39 mainly illustrate gains and losses in the P & L but for IFRS 9 due to the separation and traceability of FV changes for the P & L as well as the OCI result in a higher workload (PricewaterhouseCoopers Aktiengesellschaft Wirtschaftsprüfungs-gesellschaft 2017a, 561 and 1137; Horngren et al. 2014, 65).

5.2 Deposits from banks

In regard to deposits from banks, the characteristics are similar to deposits from customers. However, the focus is set on the interaction with non-banks and the interbank trading with other credit institutions (Hartmann-Wendels, Pfingsten and Weber 2015, 213).

5.2.1 Terms and conditions

Regarding the terms and conditions, deposits from banks differ from those of customers. Besides the costs of the deposit from customers that need to be considered, another point to bear in mind is that in the most cases the deposit has an undefined maturity and might not directly be exposed to the market rates. Therefore, assumptions are made in order to replicate a portfolio with rolling maturities. In contrast to that, deposits from banks are assessed in line with the residual maturity (Gentili and Santini 2014, 90f.). While banks might earn an interest margin, it is reasonable to assume that volatile economic situations are associated with changes in the interest rate and therefore require the risks in the banking book to be managed as a mismatch between short-term funding and long-term lending occurs (Choudhry 2007, 249).

Furthermore, deposits from customers are affected by the maturity transformation and thus the effect of interest rate changes. Therefore, banks profit from short-term rates at which they obtain funds and lend it to customers at a higher rate. If the short-term interest rate is below the long-term interest rate, which initially is higher than the short-term interest rate, the bank might generate a profit. However, if this is the opposite, the bank needs to have enough liquidity for withdrawals. Consequently, the bank must manage interest rate and the liquidity risk in order to maintain enough cash reserves for the customers. Apart from the fact that the bank is obligated to have a deposit guarantee scheme which requests to hold cash in accordance with the CRR, the bank also focuses on holding financial instruments and obtaining funds in the market to generate return. Such financial instruments are derivatives, forward rate agreements, swaps or hedge instruments (Choudhry 2007, 248f.).

5.2.2 Influencing factors and impact factors

As for deposits from customers, ALM also manages the risk arising from deposits from banks. Apart from the previously discussed influencing and impact factors on the customer side, the focus in this chapter is set on the gap analysis for deposits of banks. The gap analysis focuses on the interest rate risk which occurs from the banking book, consequently positions held in the trading book are not affected. Due to a mismatch between the interest rates, a bank faces basis risk. For instance, a bank uses a prime rate for the loans but refinances itself using an indexed interest rate such as the EURIBOR. However, it occurs for deposits from customers that the yield is lower than the interest rate used in the fund transfer pricing. A bank is also exposed to the basis risk using derivative instruments. Consequently, a swap that contains two floating rates, e.g. the six-month-EURIBOR and three-month-EURIBOR to which a basis spread as the difference between the two floating rates is added (Gentili and Santini 2014, 86ff.).

Regarding the gap analysis, the aim is to determine the effect on the NII when the yield curve shifts. The gap is the difference between rate sensitive assets, liabilities and off-balance-sheet items. As a result, the decisive factor is the interest rate and therefore it is distinguished between a positive and negative gap. The positive gap occurs when assets are more interest rate sensitive than liabilities. The negative gap happens when interest rate sensitive liabilities outweigh the assets. Assuming that the interest rate rises and the banking book is positively gapped, NII increases and conversely. If the banking book is negatively gapped, the interest rate changes impact the NII in the contrary way. Besides the interest rate, the maturity is essential as certain assets and liabilities are grouped in line with the maturity (Choudhry 2007, 258f.; Gentili and Santini 2014, 90).

For the gap analysis, assumptions are made. First, it is assumed that the yield curve only shifts parallelly which might deviate in practice resulting from the basis risk. Second, the repayment schedules are not adapted. From a theoretical point of view, a bank demands customer to pay interest and capital on a loan regardless if a low-interest period exists. Finally, the repricing of both the asset and liability side is conducted in the middle of the corresponding maturity bucket. Regarding the advantages and disadvantages, banks are able to conduct the gap analysis easily also illustrating financial positions which are affected by the interest rate change. Based on this, a bank reviews instruments for the hedging purpose and limits. However, the disadvantage is in the maturity bucket due to mismatch of assets and liabilities and affects the NII unexpectedly. Moreover, the parallel shift hinders banks to use the gap analysis for embedded options when applying caps and floors for the interest rates (Choudhry 2007, 259; Gentili and Santini 2014, 92f.).

5.2.3 Measurement

Due to the fact that the measurement of deposits from banks is conform to deposits from customers, the most relevant factors are briefly summarised and the examples described in the previous chapter are considered. The initial recognition and derecognition is equal to deposits from customers using IAS 39 and IFRS 9. In terms of IAS 39, deposits from banks are initially measured at AC and the effective interest rate method is used. Nevertheless, the FVO is exercisable in case of an accounting mismatch. In terms of IAS 39, deposits from banks are recognised at the FV. Moreover, the utilisation of the effective interest rate method requires disagios/agios and accrued interest to be considered. Regarding the valuation of embedded derivatives, it remains the same as for deposits from customers. In contrast to that, IFRS 9 is unchanged to IAS 39 apart from the measurement of the FVO which aims to separate the default risk from the general market risks by transferring the amount into the OCI, consequently, affecting the balance sheet and the amount of equity. As for deposits from customers, also deposits from banks are requested to use the P & L and OCI when deciding for the FVO (PricewaterhouseCoopers Aktiengesellschaft Wirtschaftsprüfungsgesellschaft 2017b, 1919ff.).

5.3 Own issuance

When a bank decides to issue a bond, it aims to refinance itself through debt. This kind of securitisation differentiates from shares as they represent own equity with no fixed maturity and dividend payments attributable to the economic situation of the bank. Regarding the term, bonds issued below the period of one year tend to be considered short-term while maturities above one year are long-term. This separation also leads to the distinction of money and capital market. However, it is reasonable to assume that the capital market instruments are of higher importance as banks aim to refinance themselves for a longer period (Enthofer and Haas 2016, 385 and 387; Mishkin 2016, 71ff. and 75).

5.3.1 Terms and conditions

To begin with, bonds offer advantages to investors and issuers. The investors lend money to e.g. a bank and receive interest and the principal amount invested at maturity. In regard to bonds, there are some specific terms used and the most relevant ones are described in this chapter. While there are many issuers, the focus is set on banks as issuing institution. Another point to consider is the maturity of a bond which defines the date at which the last coupon and the initially invested principal is paid to the investor. Additionally, the term face or par value is of relevance as the redemption is quoted in percentage of the face value. Therefore, redemption is at 100 % of the face value, whereas the issuance might be below or above the face value of 1,000. Besides the maturity and face value, the coupon is of interest for the investor. As for the redemption, also the quotation of the coupon is quoted as a percentage of the face value, e.g. 3 % on a face value of 1,000 equals a coupon payment of 30. Depending on the bond, it pays either a fixed or a variable coupon for which an appropriate interest reference rate is indicated. In addition to the coupon, the bank adds a spread that represents the quoted margin and results in the difference between the bid/ask price. In contrast, the yield to maturity is the average rate of return for a bond bought by the investor and held until maturity. Consequently, the paid coupons are reinvested and a compound interest is received. Generally, a bank offers fixed, variable or zero bonds but also issues special types of bonds e.g. convertible bonds or index-linked bonds. Commonly used are fixed bonds also known as plain-vanilla-bonds although the interest rate risk is higher for fixed than for variable bonds – called floating rate notes. However, zero bonds are issued below par, pay no coupon and are redeemed above par, thereby compensating for the coupon payments left during the maturity (Mobius 2012, 3 and 85 and 88; Mondello 2017, 407ff. and 413 and 417f. and 422).

With reference to the issuance of bonds, the present value is an essential component of measurement since the value of money, e.g. 100 Euro differs from today and a one-year-perspective as interest is earned at a bank deposit. Consequently, the present value of a bond is the cash flows – coupon and redemption payment – which are discounted by the interest rate for the duration of the investment (Mishkin 2016, 110f.). In regard to the type of bond, the terminology of accrued interest and the difference between clean and dirty price is described. While the clean price is the price without considering the accrued interest, the dirty price is the price paid by the investor including accrued interest (Choudhry 2007, 162).

Before describing how the pricing is determined, the emission of the bond is stated. Regarding the issuance of bonds, a bank uses the primary market for the first issuance while on the secondary market already issued bonds are traded on the stock exchange or OTC. For the secondary market the pricing evolves from supply and demand. In terms of the primary market and a company that intends to issue a bond, it is possible to take advantage of an underwriting consortium that engages a bank or the company itself to issue bonds for refinancing purposes. From a banking point of view, the issuance is less complicated. Apart from the underwriting consortium and own issuance, the third possibility is a tender procedure where a minimum price is set by the bank and investors offer the price and quantity they wish to purchase until the issuing volume is reached (Mondello 2017, 444ff. and 447).

In regard to the pricing and measurement, financial liabilities are measured at AC according to IFRS 9.4.2.1 and 9.5.3.1 unless exercising the FVO. Using the measurement at AC, bonds are recorded at the FV considering also transaction costs. As for the FV measurement, the FV hierarchy contains three levels in order to evaluate the FV. First of all, level one called mark-to-market obtains the FV from similar assets. Secondly, level two known as mark-to-model is a valuation model to assess the FV applying input factors, e.g. the development of interest rates or the creditworthiness of the bank. Finally, level three is the mark-to-management approach that is used if level one and two are not applicable. As a result, the bond is judged on the observable factors available and by applying adequate valuations models. In terms of AC it is assumed that the bond issued is held until maturity and shows no changes in the interest rate. Therefore, unpredictable changes in the interest rate lead to a change in the value of the bond. However, this adjustment is not shown in the balance sheet as the measurement is at AC (Massari, Gianfrate and Zanetti 2014, 22; Rose and Hudgins 2013, 142ff; Wagenhofer 2018, 508 and 511).

5.3.2 Influencing factors and impact factors

Regarding the influencing factors on the market price of the bond, common factors are the time until the bonds matures, the current market yield for a similar bond and the yield set for the bond bought, credit and liquidity risk for bonds intended to be sold on secondary markets (Enthofer and Haas 2016, 397).

Generally, bonds are less risky than shares for investors. Thus, the bank might not pay out dividends but is still obliged to repay the redemption and coupon. However, this chapter outlines the risks bonds are exposed to and which impact and influence it has on the treatment of own issuances. A crucial factor is the interest rate risk. In general, long-term bonds are more risky than short-term bonds as the probability of interest rate changes in the long term is higher, also influencing fixed bonds. In accordance with supply and demand, there is an interaction between interest rates and bond prices. Consequently, if interest rates rise (fall), the bond price falls (rises) as investors choose the more attractive interest. This affects straight bonds with a fixed yield as it is solely exposed to changes in the price and therby leads in the adaption of the bond price (Mobius 2012, 95f.; Mondello 2017, 406 and 506).

Apart from using the effective rate of interest for discounting cash flows, the bank might use spot rates or forward rates. In order to use the spot rates, the rates can either be obtained from the capital market or zero bonds with the maturity needed. As a zero bond pays no coupon, the effective interest rate is assessed by dividing the redemption payment by the price to the square of one considering maturity. Moreover, the forward rate is calculated for e.g. the first year using the spot rates in the first and second year. Nevertheless, the availability of zero bonds is not always fulfilled and therefore the usage of swaps is recommendable (Heidorn and Schäffler 2017, 42ff. and 46).

Another point to consider, especially regarding the IFRS 9 measurement, is the credit spread risk. The credit spread risk refers to the difference between a bond's yield and the interest reference rate but is also the loss occurred while the creditworthiness of the issuer remains unchanged (Enthofer and Haas 2016, 1049 and 1071). In order to evaluate the credit spread of bonds, three approaches are offered: the asset swap prices, yield to maturity calculation and the zero curve. The asset swap prices method is used to settle differences in rates when a bond is bought at 100. However, deviations from 100 lead to difficulties in the measurement of a bonds credit spread as the credit spread of the asset swap counterparty is missing (Enthofer and Haas 2016, 1055 and 1061). Secondly, the yield to maturity calculation is a simple approach to conduct as an Excel formula is used under the condition that an interest reference rate is comparable to a bonds maturity. Nevertheless, the prerequisite is a flat interest curve and no reinvestment risk. Finally, the zero curve is shifted to determine the credit spread of bonds which aims to lead the bonds yield curve to approximate to the yield of the market price (Enthofer and Haas 2016, 1061 and 1063).

5.3.3 Measurement

In regard to the measurement of debt securities issued by banks, the approach is similar to deposits from customers. The objective is to explain how the results are influenced by IAS 39 and IFRS 9. In accordance with IAS 1.54(m), financial liabilities are required to be separated in the balance sheet whereas no standard deals with securitised debt. However, as for deposits from customers also securitised debt is due to the materiality requested to be shown in the balance sheet as an item (IFRS 7.8(f)). Moreover, it is necessary to include sub-items in case of various arrangements of the bonds. As bonds include the payment of the nominal amount as well as the coupons, they are considered as debt instrument and thereby not as equity. Beginning with the measurement in line with IAS 39, bonds are initially recognised if the bond becomes part of a contractual agreement (IAS 39.14). The derecognition is consistent with deposits from customers. Furthermore, the derecognition of debt instruments is also conducted for buy-backs of the issuer. Therefore, the amount which results from the difference of the acquisition cost and the book value is recorded in the P & L. Regarding the topic of disagio/agio, accrued interest and the separation of embedded derivatives due to the right of cancellation, the approach remains as described for deposits from customers (PricewaterhouseCoopers Aktiengesellschaft Wirtschaftsprüfungsgesellschaft 2017a, 532 and 714ff.; PricewaterhouseCoopers Aktiengesellschaft Wirtschaftsprüfungsgesellschaft 2017b, 1935ff.).

The measurement of bonds issued by the bank is at AC unless the FVO is exercised. At the initial recognition, the issued bond is measured at the FV which equals the face value including transaction costs. However, assuming the bank issues a bond of 1 million, it is not placing the entire amount but rather sells step-by-step based on the accrued interest. With reference to table seven, the subsequent measurement for bonds issued at AC is set by the calculation of the effective interest rate which solely considers disagios/agios and derecognition in the P & L. With reference to example eight referring to the measurement at FVTPL, the approach is conform for the issuance of bonds. Hence, the credit risk and all other changes in the FV are booked into the P & L (PricewaterhouseCoopers Aktiengesellschaft Wirtschaftsprüfungsgesellschaft 2017b, 1938f.).

In terms of the measurement applying IFRS 9, the initial recognition and derecognition of issued bonds is unchanged (PricewaterhouseCoopers Aktiengesellschaft Wirtschaftsprüfungsgesellschaft 2017a, 532 and 1037; PricewaterhouseCoopers Aktiengesellschaft Wirtschaftsprüfungsgesellschaft 2017b, 714ff and 1047f.). In line with IFRS 9, the issuance of bonds measured at AC is carried out with the effective interest rate method. Moreover, the measurement at FVTPL follows the method described in the example in table nine. As for the two previously described financial liabilities, own issuances are measured at AC and solely affect the P & L. While this is consistent with the FVO applying IAS 39, IFRS 9 records the FV change in the P & L and splits the part which belongs to creditworthiness of the bank and books it against the OCI as part of the equity (PricewaterhouseCoopers Aktiengesellschaft Wirtschafts-prüfungsgesellschaft 2017a, 589):

Example – Issuance of bonds measured at FVTPL (IFRS 9)

31.12.2001: Bank issues a bond with a nominal amount of 10 million (face value 1,000 and 10,000 bonds) at par maturing in two years. Coupon rate is 10 % paid semi-annually.

Cash / Bonded debt	10 million

Interest payment to debt holders, twice a year for two years in total (totalling to 2 million)

Interest expense (P & L) / Cash	500,000

Redemption payment at maturity

Bonded Debt / Cash	10 million

Scenario 1: Credit risk decreases from 2 % to 1 %

Bonded debt / Gain FVTPL (P & L)	1 million
Gain FVTPL / Accumulated OCI	1 million

Scenario 2: Credit risk increases from 1 % to 2 %	
Loss FVTPL (P & L) / Bonded debt	1 million
Accumulated OCI / Loss FVTPL	1 million

Table 10 | Example – Issuance of bonds measured at FVTPL (IFRS 9)

(Source: PricewaterhouseCoopers Aktiengesellschaft Wirtschaftsprüfungs-gesellschaft 2017a, 589 and 1123; Horngren et al. 2014, 422)

5.4 Annual statement analysis

The empirical analysis of this master thesis is to examine the results of the financial statements of RBI AG and Erste Group AG regarding the FV measurement of deposits from customers, deposits from banks and own issuances. Moreover, the measurement of the own default risk is reviewed. As IFRS 9 are effective since January 1 of 2018, the analysis is conducted for the following financial statements of RBI AG and Erste Group AG: the annual report of 2017, the annual report of 2018 and the first quarterly report of 2019 of the consolidated financial statements respectively the interim consolidated financial statements for the first quarter of 2019. Erste Group AG and RBI AG are categorised as significant institutions (SIs) in terms of the Single Supervisory Mechanism (SSM). The SSM is a banking supervision lead by the European Central Bank (ECB) and national supervisory authorities with the objective to ensure stability in the financial system. Furthermore, Erste Group AG and RBI AG are also directly supervised by the ECB due to the size of the total assets - Erste Group AG owns total assets that amount to EUR 150-300 billion whereas RBI AG records total assets in the amount of EUR 100-150 billion as per 1 June 2019 (European Central Bank 2019, 20f.; Oesterreichische Nationalbank 2018, 27).

5.4.1 Raiffeisen Bank International Aktiengesellschaft

The following topics of RBI AG financial statements are analysed for the financial year 2017 and 2018 as well as for the quarterly report of 2019 (Raiffeisen Bank International AG 2018, 79):

- statement of comprehensive income
- statement of financial position
- statement of financial position according to the measurement categories
- composition of each liability
- breakdown of maturities

RBI AG describes the effect of IFRS 9 in its annual report 2017. As a result, equity is approximately reduced by EUR 230 million due to impairment requirements whereas an increase of equity in the amount of EUR 70 million is related to the classification and measurement. The figures of the financial statements in 2017 and 2018 are illustrated in Euro thousand whereas the quarterly report of 2019 shows the figures in Euro million (Raiffeisen Bank International AG 2018, 235).

The following chapter examines the consequences of moving from AC to FV measurement and the impact of the own default risk of RBI AG. Beginning with the consolidated financial statements of 2017, it is necessary to emphasise the merge of Raiffeisen Zentralbank Österreich AG and RBI AG which is illustrated in the financial results 2017. However, the financial results from 2016 are solely from RBI AG leading to less comparability. In addition, RBI AG applied IFRS 9.7.1.2 which prescribes the presentation of financial liabilities measured at FVTPL (Raiffeisen Bank International AG 2018, 80f.; Wagenhofer 2018, 524f.).

As the presentation of financial liabilities measured at FVTPL is already applied in the financial year 2017, the changes due to the default risk of RBI AG are included in the statement other comprehensive income and total comprehensive income. It is distinguished between the OCI where income and expenses directly affect equity and the OCI that is afterwards transferred into the P & L. While FV changes resulting from the default risk of RBI AG are booked into the P & L amounting to a loss of EUR 119,064 in 2016, the changes in the FV are assigned into the OCI instead of the P & L in 2017. Therefore, under the section items which are not reclassified to profit and loss, the FV changes of financial liabilities at fair value through profit or loss attributable to changes in their default risk show a minus of EUR 139,643 which accounts from group equity in 2017 whereas the comparable figure for 2016 is zero indicating that changes are booked into the P & L prior to that. In contrast, the default risk of RBI AG due to the FVO within retained earnings amounts to EUR 75,591 for the beginning of 2017. Due to the loss of EUR 139,643, the cumulative change in the FV is a negative EUR 64,052. The amount of EUR 597,508 is due to the difference between the FV of liabilities for which the FVO is chosen and the contractual amount to be paid. With the early adoption of the presentation of financial liabilities measured at FVTPL, RBI AG aims to decrease an accounting mismatch as assets measured at FV are not adequate to the measurement of liabilities thereby affecting the income statement (Raiffeisen Bank International AG 2018, 80ff. and 233ff.).

While the presentation and transfer of the own default risk into the OCI is in line with IFRS 9, initial recognition and subsequent measurement are exercised in accordance with IAS 39. Generally, the FV for the initial recognition is either obtained from the market as an observable price or assessed through a valuation technique or pricing model. Financial instruments for which the measurement is conducted at FVTPL, the FV determined includes market risk factors and the issuers credit risk. The result of the measurement for financial instruments at FVTPL is shown in the income statement as net income from derivatives and liabilities. While RBI AG incurred a loss of EUR 188,752 in 2016, the results improved significantly as the loss amounts solely EUR 40,921 in 2017. Considering the items that account for the total net income of derivatives and liabilities, the net income from liabilities designated at FV reflects the change in market interest rates totalling to EUR 62,831 in 2017 whereas the year before it showed a loss of EUR 105,078. This loss is attributable to the own default risk of RBI AG amounting to EUR 119,064 and a relatively low net income of EUR 13,986 due to market interest rates (Raiffeisen Bank International AG 2018, 80 and 98 and 103 and 218f.).

Regarding the FV measurement, the FV hierarchy is of relevance for the assessment of the FV and the reporting of RBI AG. If possible, the FV is determined by external data sources. This occurs especially for level one since this level considers quoted prices which RBI AG applies on listed securities, derivatives and liquid bonds on the OTC market. Other than that, level two contains financial instruments for which no market price is set. For this case, RBI AG uses financial instruments that are similarly or valuation models – such as the present value calculation or option pricing model for which market data e.g. reproducible yield curves, credit spreads and volatilities – are obtained. Financial instruments that belong to this level are OTC-derivatives and non-quoted debt instruments. Finally, financial instruments are categorised into level three of the FV hierarchy as there is no ability to access market data. Instead historical data is used and adapted and mainly relies on the assumptions made that differ in regard to complexity and transparency of a financial instrument. Level three affects credit spreads derived from internal estimates. Nevertheless, RBI AG sets in its recognition and measurement principles the focus on AC as most financial liabilities are assessed at AC (Raiffeisen Bank International AG 2018, 140 and 222).

With respect to the consolidated financial statements of 2018, the same topics are covered as for 2017. Therefore, the statement of comprehensive income is described and the three liabilities are examined in the corresponding chapter. The financial statements of 2018 highlight IFRS 9 and the presentation of the statements of financial position but also the comparable period and its reporting date that is conducted in line with the financial reporting standards (FINREP) initiated by the European Banking Authority. Further, RBI AG did not adapt the comparative information of the previous periods in regard to classification and measurement changes. Moreover, the measurement of debt instruments that are categorised into the business model to collect, must meet the condition of the SPPI criterion, thereby indicating that the subsequent measurement is at AC unless the FVO is exercised (Raiffeisen Bank International AG 2019a, 86 and 104f.).

Regarding the statement of comprehensive income, the other comprehensive income and total comprehensive income differentiate between items which are not reclassified to profit or loss and items that might be reclassified to profit or loss. The former includes FV changes resulting from the credit risk of financial liabilities which opt in for the FVO. This position indicates a recovery from a loss of EUR 139,643 in 2017 to EUR 33,692 in 2018 that remains in the OCI. Instead of the movement from AC to FV, RBI AG reclassified financial liabilities designated at FV to AC, thereby occurring a carrying amount of EUR 447,781. This reclassification lead to the positive figure of EUR 33,692 and a considerable decrease in FV changes traceable back to the default risk of RBI AG. As a result, the difference between liabilities designated at FV and the amount contractually to be paid is minus EUR 404,000 in 2018 (Raiffeisen Bank International AG 2019a, 88). The statement of changes in equity includes changes in equity and cumulative other comprehensive income which shows the unrealised net gain of EUR 33,692. In regard to the changes in equity, IFRS 9 lead to a decrease in equity of minus EUR 169,438 of which EUR 69,938 are accounted for previously at FV designated deposits and debt instruments (Raiffeisen Bank International AG 2019a, 91f).

With reference to the income statement, which is part of the comprehensive income, the net trading income and FV result is adapted in line with IFRS 9. Consequently, a substantial decrease from EUR 35,473 in 2017 to EUR 16,890 is illustrated in 2018. Regardless of the development of assets, the net trading income and FV result is split into net gains/losses on financial assets and liabilities – held for trading and net gains/losses on financial assets and liabilities – designated at FVTPL. Each of this category illustrates deposits, debt securities issued and other financial liabilities. Deposits held for trading decreased tremendously from minus EUR 128 in 2017 to minus EUR 53,215 in 2018 whereas deposits at FVTPL slightly decreased from EUR 12,426 in 2017 to EUR 11,002 in 2018. For debt securities issued that are held for trading the gains amount to EUR 682 in 2017 and decreased considerably to a loss of EUR 797 in 2018 while debt securities issued at FVTPL remain positive, the amount of EUR 48,974 in 2017 decreased to EUR 16,148 in 2018. For other financial liabilities held for trading, an increase from EUR 1,710 in 2017 to EUR 5,427 is shown in 2018. In contrast, other financial liabilities at FVTPL amount to EUR 112 while the financial statement of 2018 showed a result of zero (Raiffeisen Bank International AG 2019a, 87 and 119f.). In regard to other net operating income, gains/losses on derecognition of financial assets and liabilities – not measured at FVTPL slightly improved. Deposits incurred a loss of EUR 2,233 in 2017 while the result for 2018 is zero. Similarly, other financial liabilities amount to minus EUR 1,487 in 2017 and amount zero in 2018. In contrast to that, debt securities issued indicated a loss of EUR 407 in 2017 and deteriorated to minus EUR 983 in 2018 (Raiffeisen Bank International AG 2019a, 121).

With the new presentation of the statement of financial position, the term changed into financial liabilities – amortised cost, financial liabilities – designated fair value through profit/loss and financial liabilities – held for trading. Due to IFRS 9, RBI AG illustrates the effect of the standards on the carrying amount. While financial liabilities – designated at FVTPL are impacted by reclassifications and remeasurements, financial liabilities at AC are solely affected through reclassification and equity through remeasurements. In contrast to that, IFRS 9 did not affect financial liabilities held for trading (Raiffeisen Bank International AG 2019a, 112):

Equity and liabilities in EUR thousand	IAS 39 Carrying amount 31/12/2017	Re-classifications	Re-measurements	IFRS 9 Carrying amount 1/1/2018
Financial liabilities – AC	EUR 114,794,111	EUR 447,781	EUR 0	EUR 115,241,892
Financial liabilities – designated FVTPL	EUR 2,508,622	EUR (447,781)	EUR (69,938)	EUR 1,990,903
Financial liabilities – held for trading	EUR 4,414,477	EUR 0	EUR 0	EUR 4,414,477
Equity	EUR 11,241,350	EUR 0	EUR (169,438)	EUR 11,071,912

Table 11 | RBI AG - IFRS 9 Transition

(Source: Raiffeisen Bank International AG 2019a, 112)

Regarding the FV measurement, the approach is conform with the consolidated financial statements 2017. For financial liabilities held for trading, the recognition is at FV and is either assessed by obtainable market prices or valuation models. For financial liabilities designated at FVTPL, changes in the own credit risk are recorded in the OCI. Finally, for the majority of financial liabilities which are measured at AC, the effective interest rate method as in 2017 is utilised. Consequently, financial liabilities – amortised cost are measured at AC and belong to the category AC in line with IFRS 9. Financial liabilities – designated FV through profit/loss and financial liabilities – held for trading are both measured at FV in line with IFRS 9 and are categorised as FVTPL. While in the consolidated financial statements 2017 each liability is evaluated for the remaining maturity, the consolidated financial statements of 2018 solely reflect the remaining maturity for the financial positions: financial liabilities – amortised cost, financial liabilities – designated fair value through profit/loss and financial liabilities – held for trading. For financial liabilities measured at AC which are due at call or without maturity, decreased significantly by EUR 8,102,920 to EUR 59,228,519 in 2018. In contrast, financial liabilities at AC that have a maturity up to three months rose by EUR 2,554,350 to EUR 17,406,300 in 2018 and more than three months but up to one year increased by EUR 1,774,968 to EUR 13,434,188 in 2018. Another considerable increase is attributable to long-term financial liabilities at AC that are more than one year but up to five years that rose by EUR 8,123,644 to a total of EUR 22,372,904 in 2018. Finally, the maturity of more than five years decreased slightly to EUR 6,632,187 in 2018. For financial liabilities designated at FVTPL the amount for due at call or without maturity decreased from EUR 10,000 in 2017 to zero in 2018. For liabilities up to three months and more than three months but up to one year showed a slight decrease that lead to EUR 142,574 and EUR 265,799 respectively in 2018. Another decrease is indicated for long term liabilities that are more than one year but up to five years, leading to a fall of EUR 558,259 totalling to EUR 975,203 in 2018. The liabilities at FVTPL for which the maturity is above five years increased by EUR 92,361 to EUR 547,500 in 2018. Finally, as with the previous both categories, also financial liabilities – held for trading show a decrease of EUR 242,587 leading to EUR 133,755 in 2018 for liabilities due at call or without maturity. Both, up to three months and more than three months but up to one year increased by EUR 294,176 and EUR 282,706 totalling to EUR 641,450 and EUR 800,200 respectively for 2018. Additionally, the long-term liabilities held for trading grew slightly by EUR 103,696 for the term of more than one year but up to five years and by EUR 129,366 for the maturity exceeding five years totalling to EUR 2,362,179 and EUR 1,164,251 respectively (Raiffeisen Bank International AG 2019a, 90 and 150 and 176f. and 246ff.).

The final financial statements to be analysed for RBI AG is the interim consolidated financial statements as at 31 March 2019 (Q1 2019). One relevant aspect is that the consolidated financial statements of 2017 and 2018 are presented in Euro thousand whereas the interim report is stated in Euro million. The following topics are covered: statement of comprehensive income, net trading income and other net operating income as well as the statement of changes in equity (Raiffeisen Bank International AG 2019b, 32).

To begin with, the statement of comprehensive income which consists of the income statement and other comprehensive income and total comprehensive income is described. The income statement includes the net trading income and FV result for Q1 2019 which amounts to a loss of EUR 52. In contrast, the loss of Q1 2018 amounted solely to EUR 1 leading to an increase of more than 500 %. This circumstance is caused by derivatives held for economic hedging purposes that expect to be offset during the maturity of the portfolio. The net trading income and FV result is as for the consolidated financial statements in 2018 split into net gains/losses on financial assets and liabilities – held for trading and net gains/losses on financial assets and liabilities – designated at fair value through profit/loss. For deposits, the net loss – held for trading increased substantially from EUR 1 in Q1 2018 to minus EUR 14 in Q1 2019. Debt securities issued changed from EUR 2 in Q1 2018 to zero in Q1 2019, while other financial liabilities remained constant. However, both deposits and debt securities issued – designated at FVTPL showed a loss in Q1 2019 compared to Q1 2018. Deposits amounting to EUR 7 dropped to minus EUR 2 and debt securities issued amounting to EUR 6 decreased to minus EUR 6 in Q1 2019 respectively. Other net operating income of RBI AG resulted in a profit of EUR 4 in Q1 2019 for gains/losses on the derecognition of financial assets and liabilities not measured at FVTPL. However, a decrease exists compared to EUR 16 in Q1 2018 which is attributable to the sale of registered bonds. For other comprehensive income and total comprehensive income as part of the statement of comprehensive income, FV changes occurred through the credit risk of financial liabilities not being reclassified into the P & L recovered to EUR 4 in Q1 2019 whereas it amounts to minus EUR 1 in Q1 2018 (Raiffeisen Bank International AG 2019b, 9 and 33f. and 50f.).

Furthermore, the statement of changes in equity shows the development for the period from 1 January 2019 to 31 March 2019 leading to an increase in retained earnings (EUR 226) and cumulative OCI (EUR 154). In contrast, total comprehensive income for the period from January until March 2018 amounts to EUR 399 whereas a loss of EUR 30 is assigned to the cumulative OCI (Raiffeisen Bank International AG 2019b, 36). In regard to the measurement at FVTPL, the difference between the FV and contractually to be paid amounts to minus EUR 404 at the end of 2018 and decreased to minus EUR 406 for Q1 2019 (Raiffeisen Bank International AG 2019b, 61).

5.4.1.1 Deposits from customers

For deposits from customers the statement of financial position, the measurement category, the composition of deposits from customers and the breakdown of the maturities is described for 2017, 2018 and 2019. Deposits from customers listed in the statement of financial position of RBI AG show an increase from EUR 71,538,226 in 2016 to 84,831,440 in 2017. As of first January 2017, the amount of EUR 8,786,770 is already included attributable to the merger (Raiffeisen Bank International AG 2018, 84 and 96).

The section notes to the statement of financial position illustrate an overview on RBI AG financial positions according to the measurement categories. Regarding equity and liabilities, the relevant measurement categories for liabilities are trading liabilities, financial liabilities and liabilities at fair value through profit and loss. As a matter of fact, deposits from customers listed in the section financial liabilities indicate the measurement at AC and thereby is in line with IFRS 7 and IAS 39. However, the FV of deposits from customers is determined by RBI AG if a remaining maturity of more than one year for fixed interest exists and an interest rate adjustment period of more than one year is set for variable interest. The FV exceeds the book value by EUR 41,775 which implies a higher FV of deposits from customers than its carrying amount. The composition of the FV of deposits from customers is split between the three levels of the FV hierarchy. While level one remains zero, level two amounts to EUR 27,859,894 and level three, based on assumptions, reaches a total of EUR 57,013,321. The reason for deposits from customers categorised in level three is the low trading activity. RBI AG uses fair value hedges for the purpose of managing interest rate risks for deposits from customers based on the condition that hedge accounting as regulated in IAS 39 is applicable. Thereby, the amounts in both 2016 and 2017 reflect the book value changes due to hedging (Raiffeisen Bank International AG 2018, 108f. and 112 and 140f. and 144 and 220ff. and 223).

Regarding the type of RBI AG deposits from customers, sight deposits result in the highest amount which increased from EUR 44,461,093 in 2016 to EUR 50,414,380 in 2017. The second highest component is time deposits that decreased by EUR 220,690 to a total of EUR 23,124,190 in 2017. Finally, savings deposits attribute the smallest amount of deposits from customers. Due to the merger, RBI increased the amount of savings deposits by EUR 7,560,616 in the financial year 2017 (Raiffeisen Bank International AG 2018, 123).

Apart from the distinction regarding the types of deposits, deposits from customers are categorised in short-term liabilities and long-term liabilities. For short-term liabilities RBI AG defines three time horizons which are due at call or without maturity, up to three months and more than three months but up to one year. In contrast, long-term liabilities contain deposits from customers that are more than one year but up to five years and deposits having a maturity of more than five years. In both 2016 and 2017, deposits from customers which are due at call or have no maturity are by far the highest amount although the amount increased in 2017 by EUR 7,899,911 to a total of EUR 55,904,379. However, the longer the terms to maturity, the lower the amount of deposits from customers. Consequently, the maturity up to three months amounts to EUR 11,605,985 while a maturity of more than five years contains only EUR 1,734,609 in 2017 (Raiffeisen Bank International AG 2018, 134).

With regards to the measurement of deposits from customers, the effective interest rate method determines the AC and thereby reflects the same procedure as in the theoretical part. The future cash flows including expenses, for instance fees, are discounted by the effective interest rate over the period of the financial instrument. The result is the net carrying amount at initial recognition (Raiffeisen Bank International AG 2018, 223).

In the consolidated financial statements of 2018, RBI AG adapted the presentation of the statement of financial position. While in 2017, the item was listed as deposits from customers, financial liabilities are categorised into (Raiffeisen Bank International AG 2019a, 90):

- Financial liabilities – amortised cost
- Financial liabilities – designated fair value through profit/loss
- Financial liabilities – held for trading

Due to IFRS 9 and the new presentation, RBI AG illustrated the adaption presented at 31 December 2017 and 1 January 2017 (Raiffeisen Bank International AG 2019a, 107 and 109):

Equity and liabilities 31/12/2017 in EUR thousand	Deposits from customers
Financial liabilities – amortised cost	EUR 84,831,440
Financial liabilities – designated FVTPL	EUR 0
Financial liabilities – held for trading	EUR 0
Equity and liabilities 1/1/2017 in EUR thousand	Deposits from customers
Financial liabilities – amortised cost	EUR 79,573,276
Financial liabilities – designated FVTPL	EUR 751,720
Financial liabilities – held for trading	EUR 0

Table 12 | RBI AG - Reconciliation of deposits from customers

(Source: Raiffeisen Bank International AG 2019a, 107 and 109)

For the transition of financial liabilities designated at FVTPL, RBI AG differentiates between deposits, debt securities issued and other financial liabilities which are not affected. It is reasonable to assume that deposits focus solely on deposits from customers. Generally, the FVO aims to prevent or reduce an accounting mismatch. For the transition, financial liabilities, previously reclassified to the measurement at FVTPL, are reversed to AC due to previously at FV designated debt instruments leading to minus EUR 70,800. Additionally, an amount of minus EUR 15,271 is allocated to remeasurements of financial liabilities. As a result, the weighted effective interest rate for the reclassification amounts 5 %. RBI AG illustrated the effect of the transition for deposits as follows (Raiffeisen Bank International AG 2019a, 116):

in EUR thousand	IAS 39 Carrying amount 31/12/2017	Reclassi- ficiation	Remeasure- ments	IFRS 9 Carrying amount 1/1/2018	Retained Earnings	Cumulative OCI 1/1/2018
Deposits	EUR 616,867	EUR (70,800)	EUR (15,271)	EUR 530,796	EUR 12,445	EUR 2,826
Elected subtractions to financial liabilities – AC	EUR 0	EUR (70,800)	EUR (15,271)	EUR 0	EUR 12,445	EUR 2,826

Table 13 | RBI AG - Transition financial liabilities - designated at FVTPL (Deposits)

(Source: Raiffeisen Bank International AG 2019a, 116)

In regard to financial liabilities measured at AC, deposits from customers increased from EUR 84,466,663 in 2017 to EUR 86,623,218 in 2018 and lead to the overall increase in financial liabilities measured at AC. The items that belong to deposits from customers are current accounts/overnight deposits/redeemable at notice that changed slightly from 2017 (EUR 57,018,666) to 2018 (EUR 58,705,626), deposits with agreed maturity that increased by EUR 357,104 to a total of EUR 27,769,768 in 2018 and repurchase agreements that show the highest increase from EUR 35,333 in 2017 to EUR 147,825 in 2018 (Raiffeisen Bank International AG 2019a, 139). The second measurement category are financial liabilities designated at FVTPL and are significantly lower than those measured at AC. Deposits from customers measured at FVTPL decreased from EUR 507,453 in 2017 to EUR 414,852 in 2018 solely affecting deposits with agreed maturity. Due to the nature, deposits from customers are not listed as financial liability measured as held for trading (Raiffeisen Bank International AG 2019a, 140).

With respect to the FV measurement, no distinction is set for deposits from customers and deposits from banks. Consequently, it is reasonable to assume that the levels of the FV hierarchy reflect deposits from customers. Regarding financial liabilities held for trading, neither in 2017 nor in 2018 deposits are categorised within the levels. In contrast, the designation at FVTPL remains within level two for 2017 and 2018 which decreased by EUR 336,756 to a total of EUR 435,188 in 2018. Furthermore, the FV is determined for liabilities that are measured at AC. For deposits, the FV in 2018 amounts to EUR 109,051,828 – solely attributable to level three which is below the carrying amount of EUR 110,583,061 (Raiffeisen Bank International AG 2019a, 152 and 155).

With respect to the interim consolidated financial statements of the first quarter in 2019, the following topics are discussed: statement of financial position and the topic of FV measurement for deposits. While the possibility of comparing each liability in respect to the measurement categories is difficult in 2018, the Q1 2019 report enables to review the financial liabilities separately. For deposits from customers measured at AC, the result for Q1 2019 increased slightly to a total of EUR 88,387. The items leading to the total are categorised as in 2018: current accounts/overnight deposits that decreased from EUR 58,706 at 31 December 2018 to EUR 58,649 in Q1 2019, deposits with agreed maturity increased by EUR 1,365 to EUR 29,135 in Q1 2019 and finally repurchase agreements that achieved the highest increase from EUR 148 to EUR 604 for Q1 2019. For deposits from customers designated at FVTPL a loss amounting to EUR 61 incurred, leading to a total of EUR 354 in Q1 2019 affecting solely deposits with agreed maturity (Raiffeisen Bank International AG 2019b, 60f.). In regard to the financial liabilities measured at FVTPL, RBI AG lists deposits that indicate a decrease in level two reaching EUR 379 in Q1 2019. Concerning deposits measured at AC, the FV of level three amounts to EUR 114,311 and is below the carrying amount of EUR 115,247 in Q1 2019 which remains similar to 2018 (Raiffeisen Bank International AG 2019b, 65 and 69f.).

5.4.1.2　Deposits from banks

As with deposits from customers, the statement of financial position, the measurement category, the composition of deposits from banks and the breakdown of the maturities is covered for 2017, 2018 and 2019. Starting with the consolidated financial statements of 2017, deposits from banks increased from EUR 12,816,475 in 2016 to EUR 22,291,431 in 2017. While deposits from banks amount to EUR 12,816,475 at the end of 2016, the change due to the merger is EUR 11,243,299 which results in EUR 24,059,774 for the beginning of 2017 (Raiffeisen Bank International AG 2018, 84 and 96).

While deposits from customers are measured at AC, the two measurement categories for deposits from banks are financial liabilities and liabilities at FVTPL. Deposits from banks listed in the category financial liabilities within the statement of financial position amount to EUR 12,064,755 in 2016 and grew to EUR 21,674,563 in 2017. As with deposits from customer, the amount stated is measured at AC, consequently, representing those financial instruments not reported at FV. Nevertheless, the FV is still calculated and considers fixed and variable interest above the maturity of one year or a rollover period above one year, respectively. While the FV is derived from the three levels, deposits from banks are evaluated based on level two amounting to EUR 19,493,736 and level three EUR 2,220,271. The total FV EUR 21,714,007 exceeds the carrying amount by EUR 39,444 (Raiffeisen Bank International AG 2018, 109 and 144).

The second measurement category that affects deposits from banks are the liabilities at FVTPL. It is important to point out, however, that this measurement affects a significantly lower amount. Hence, deposits from banks measured at FVTPL amount to 751,720 in 2016 and decreased to EUR 616,867 in 2017. The FV in the year 2016 and 2017 is solely traceable back to level two of the FV hierarchy which contains observable market data that is used in valuation models of RBI AG. Apart from that, deposits from banks are as deposits from customers categorised at AC in accordance to IFRS 7 and defined as financial liability in line with IAS 39 (Raiffeisen Bank International AG 2018, 109 and 140ff. and 223).

In regard to the composition, deposits from banks are divided into giro and clearing business, money market business and long-term financing. Due to the merger, giro and clearing business increased considerably from EUR 4,008,410 to EUR 11,249,519. The money market business (EUR 6,401,010 in 2017) as well as the long term-financing (EUR 4,640,902 in 2017) increased in contrast to 2016 slightly. Moreover, deposits from banks are allocated to commercial banks (EUR 19,506,475 in 2017) with the highest amount, followed by central banks (EUR 1,857,385 in 2017) and multilateral development banks (EUR 927,570 in 2017) (Raiffeisen Bank International AG 2018, 122f.).

Considering the remaining terms to maturity, the shorter the maturity, the higher the amounts. Therefore, deposits from banks indicate the highest amounts for the term due at call or without maturity. The figure grew significantly from EUR 4,084,452 in 2016 to EUR 10,578,904 in 2017. The longer the term tends to be, the lower the amounts, however, the amount of each term increased except for deposits from banks with a maturity of more than three months and up to one year (Raiffeisen Bank International AG 2018, 134).

In regard to the consolidated financial statements of 2018 and due to IFRS 9 and the new presentation, RBI AG illustrated the adaption presented at 31 December 2017 and 1 January 2017 (Raiffeisen Bank International AG 2019a, 107 and 109):

Equity and liabilities 31/12/2017 in EUR thousand	Deposits from banks
Financial liabilities – amortised cost	EUR 21,674,563
Financial liabilities – designated FVTPL	EUR 616,867
Financial liabilities – held for trading	EUR 0
Equity and liabilities 1/1/2017 in EUR thousand	Deposits from banks
Financial liabilities – amortised cost	EUR 24,059,774
Financial liabilities – designated FVTPL	EUR 0
Financial liabilities – held for trading	EUR 0

Table 14 | RBI AG - Reconciliation of deposits from banks

(Source: Raiffeisen Bank International AG 2019a, 107 and 109)

In regard to measurement categories, deposits from banks are divided into financial liabilities – amortised cost, financial liabilities – designated fair value through profit/loss and financial liabilities – held for trading. To begin with, deposits from banks categorised into financial liabilities measured at AC grew from EUR 22,268,407 in 2017 to EUR 23,959,843 in 2018. The sub-items of deposits from banks are equal to deposits from customers: current accounts/overnight deposits/redeemable at notice decreased slightly by EUR 28,761 to EUR 9,993,571 in 2018, deposits with agreed maturity rose by 1,320,688 to EUR 13,228,746 in 2018 and repurchase agreements grew by EUR 399,509 to EUR 737,526 in 2018 (Raiffeisen Bank International AG 2019a, 139). As with deposits from customers, deposits from banks are categorised into financial liabilities – designated at FVTPL indicating a significant lower amount. Deposits from banks measured at FVTPL and the sub-item deposits with agreed maturity decreased from EUR 109,414 in 2017 to solely EUR 20,336 in 2018. Deposits from banks are not listed as financial liability measured as held for trading (Raiffeisen Bank International AG 2019a, 140).

In regard to the interim consolidated financial statements of the first quarter in 2019, the statement of financial position is described. As for deposits from customers, also deposits from banks measured at AC indicate a slight increase from EUR 23,960 to EUR 26,860 in Q1 2019. The items remain the same: current accounts/overnight deposits (EUR 12,538), deposits with agreed maturity (EUR 12,067) and repurchase agreements that increased in contrast by EUR 1,517 to a total of EUR 2,255 in Q1 2019 contributing to the overall increase in the figure. However, deposits from banks with an agreed maturity designated at FVTPL increased by EU 5 to EUR 25 at the end of Q1 2019 (Raiffeisen Bank International AG 2019b, 60f.).

5.4.1.3   Own issuance

The topics discussed for own issuances is the statement of financial position, the measurement category, the composition and the breakdown of the maturities for 2017, 2018 and 2019. In regard to the own issuance of RBI AG, the statement of financial position 2017 showed a slight decrease from EUR 6,645,127 in 2016 to EUR 5,885,137 in 2017. In contrast to deposits from customers and banks, debt securities issued account for the smallest part of the merger. For 2016 the amount of EUR 6,645,127 increased by EUR 1,882,254 to EUR 8,527,381 at the start of 2017 (Raiffeisen Bank International AG 2018, 84 and 96).

Considering the measurement, debt securities issued are listed in the measurement categories financial liabilities and liabilities at FVTPL. The former category indicates a decrease from EUR 5,271,709 in 2016 to EUR 4,751,893 in 2017. As with deposits from customers and banks, the measurement is at AC. However, the FV for financial liabilities with maturities of more than one year or a rollover period of more than one year, respectively, are evaluted. It is reasonable to assume that the FV of debt securities issued derives from the three levels of the FV hierarchy whereas deposits from customers and banks are determined by level two and three. Consequently, level one amounts to solely EUR 113,056 in 2017 which is obtained by market prices. Other than that, RBI AG mainly relies on valuation models for its debt securities issued amounting to EUR 3,747,435 in 2017, followed by level three that depends on the assumptions made totalling to EUR 1,041,582. While the total FV of debt securities issued amounts to EUR 4,902,073 in 2017, the carrying amount is EUR 4,751,893 leading to the highest difference of EUR 150,180 compared to deposits that remain at a difference of approximately EUR 41,000. In addition to the measurement at AC, debt securities issued by RBI AG are also listed in the category of liabilities measured at FVTPL. However, as with deposits from banks, this part is lower than the amount measured at AC. The amount EUR 1,373,418 indicated in 2016 decreased slightly to EUR 1,133,245 in 2017 and is traceable back to level two of the FV hierarchy. According to the categories of financial instruments in IFRS 7, debt securities issued are listed as AC and financial liability on the one hand and as FV through profit and loss in line with

IAS 39 on the other hand (Raiffeisen Bank International AG 2018, 109 and 144 and 223).

For designated financial liabilities at FVTPL e.g. subordinated issues and structured bonds, RBI AG obtains market prices or applies the discounted cash flow model to measure debt securities issued. For the discounted cash flow model, cash flows are discounted by the yield curve which is adjusted by the credit spread. The credit spread is derived from similar financial instruments on the market. Moreover, market risk parameters are considered from similar financial assets (Raiffeisen Bank International AG 2018, 141 and 219).

Bonds and notes issued account for the majority of debt securities issued by RBI AG, however, it indicates a decrease from EUR 6,604,140 in 2016 to EUR 5,867,674 in 2017. While the money market instruments issued resulted in EUR 38,995 in 2016, no issuance is listed in 2017. In contrast, other debt securities issued increased from EUR 1,992 in 2016 to EUR 17,463 in 2017 (Raiffeisen Bank International AG 2018, 123).

With regards to the maturities, debt securities issued are by its characteristics defined by the termination date. As a result, debt securities issued are not due at call or without maturity. Instead, the maturity ranges from up to three months to more than five years. While the term structure remains the same as for deposits previously described, the liabilities range relatively equal. However, short-term debt securities issued for up to three months represent the smallest part amounting to EUR 495,776 whereas the maturity with more than one year but up to five years represents the highest amount of EUR 2,712,021 in 2017 (Raiffeisen Bank International AG 2018, 134).

In regard to the derecognition of financial liabilities, the repayment of obligations or the expiration but also the repurchase of bonds issued by RBI AG is considered as derecognition. The result of the derecognition is booked into the net income from derivatives and liabilities as income from repurchase of liabilities. While the repurchase of liabilities amounts to a loss of EUR 230 in 2016, the loss drastically improved to solely EUR 14 in 2017 (Raiffeisen Bank International AG 2018, 103 and 220).

With regards to the consolidated financial statements of 2018 and due to IFRS 9 and the new presentation, RBI AG illustrated the adaption presented at 31 December 2017 and 1 January 2017 (Raiffeisen Bank International AG 2019a, 107 and 109):

Equity and liabilities 31/12/2017 in EUR thousand	Debt securities issued
Financial liabilities – amortised cost	EUR 4,765,327
Financial liabilities – designated FVTPL	EUR 1,119,810
Financial liabilities – held for trading	EUR 0
Equity and liabilities 1/1/2017 in EUR thousand	Debt securities issued
Financial liabilities – amortised cost	EUR 7,153,963
Financial liabilities – designated FVTPL	EUR 1,373,418
Financial liabilities – held for trading	EUR 0

Table 15 | RBI AG - Reconciliation of debt securities issued

(Source: Raiffeisen Bank International AG 2019a, 107 and 109)

In regard to the transition of financial liabilities that are designated at FVTPL, debt securities issued include subtractions and additions from the measurement at AC. The additions from financial liabilities measured at AC amount to EUR 10,891 whereas remeasurement is EUR 104 which, however, is included in retained earnings as minus EUR 104. In contrast, the elected subtractions lead to a significant minus of EUR 387,782 in reclassification and minus EUR 54,771 for remeasurement. RBI AG illustrated the effect of the transition for debt securities as follows (Raiffeisen Bank International AG 2019a, 116):

in EUR thousand	IAS 39 Carrying amount 31/12/2017	Reclassi-fication	Remeasure-ments	IFRS 9 Carrying amount 1/1/2018	Retained Earnings	Cumulative OCI 1/1/2018
Debt securities	EUR 1,891,754	EUR (376,981)	EUR (54,667)	EUR 1,460,107	EUR (2,194)	EUR 56,860
Additions from financial liabilities – AC	EUR 0	EUR 10,891	EUR 104	EUR 0	EUR (104)	EUR 0
Elected subtractions to financial liabilities – AC	EUR 0	EUR (387,872)	EUR (54,771)	EUR 0	EUR (2,089)	EUR 56,860

Table 16 | RBI AG – Transition financial liabilities - designated at FVTPL (debt securities)

(Source: Raiffeisen Bank International AG 2019a, 116)

Debt securities issued are categorised into financial liabilities – amortised cost, financial liabilities – designated fair value through profit/loss and financial liabilities – held for trading. Debt securities issued measured at AC shows an increase of EUR 423,014 leading to a total of EUR 7,966,769 in 2018. The items that lead to this figure are certificates of deposits that significantly grew from EUR 135 in 2017 to EUR 778 in 2018, covered bonds decreasing from EUR 916,937 in 2017 to EUR 726,560 in 2018, hybrid contracts incurring a tremendous decrease from EUR 3,883 in 2017 to EUR 369 in 2018 and finally, other debt securities issued that showed an increase of EUR 616,263 totalling to EUR 7,239,063 in 2018. Moreover, other debt securities issued contain convertible compound financial instruments and non-convertible debt securities issued. The majority of the amount of EUR 7,239,063 in 2018 is attributable to non-convertible debt securities issued due to the reclassification from FVTPL to AC on the one hand and due to new issuances on the other hand (Raiffeisen Bank International AG 2019a, 139). Regarding financial liabilities – designated at FVTPL, debt securities issued represent the highest figure although the amount of EUR 1,891,754 in 2017 decreased to EUR 1,495,888 in 2018 as a reclassification at AC is conducted. In contrast to the deposits from customers or banks, debt securities issued are categorised into the third measurement category: financial liabilities – held for trading that show an increase of EUR 404,753 totalling to EUR 2,749,275 in 2018 (Raiffeisen Bank International AG 2019a, 140).

Regarding the FV categorisation, debt securities issued that are held for trading changed slightly compared to 2017. While level one contained EUR 1 in 2017, the result in 2018 is zero. Level two increased by EUR 404,897 to EUR 2,748,574 in 2018. For level three, debt securities issued decreased from EUR 826 in 2017 to EUR 700 in 2018. In contrast to that, debt securities issued considered as financial liabilities designated at FVTPL derive from level two and slightly increased to EUR 1,495,888 in 2018. It is important to point out, however, that comparability of the movement between the levels is limited due to IFRS 9 and IAS 39. As for deposits, the FV is also determined for debt securities issued measured at AC. The FV of EUR 8,267,827 – allocated to level two and three – exceeds the carrying amount of EUR 7,966,769 (Raiffeisen Bank International AG 2019a, 152f. and 155).

Finally, the interim consolidated financial statements of the first quarter in 2019 describes the statement of financial position and the development within the FV measurement. While deposits from customers and deposits from banks increased, debt securities issued, however, decreased slightly in regard to the measurement at AC. Consequently, the difference of EUR 75 led to an amount of EUR 7,892 in Q1 2019. Nevertheless, the debt securities issued which are designated at FVTPL increased by EUR 69 to a total of EUR 1,565 in Q1 2019. Moreover, an increase for debt securities issued that are held for trading of EUR 367 lead to a result of EUR 3,116 in Q1 2019 (Raiffeisen Bank International AG 2019b, 60ff.).

Additionally, debt instruments reported at FV categorised into held for trading indicate movements for the end of 2018 and Q1 2019. Level one, previously at zero in 2018, increased to EUR 52 while level three, previously EUR 1, decreased to zero in Q1 2019. The majority is categorised within level two which requires valuation models to be used and increased by EUR 316 to EUR 3,065 in Q1 2019. The measurement executed at FVTPL is solely attributable to level two which slightly increased to EUR 1,565 in Q1 2019. Furthermore, debt securities issued that are measured at AC but are not reported at FV are also shown within the interim consolidated financial statements. Level two amounting to EUR 7,642 and level three EUR 520 lead to a higher FV (EUR 8,162) than the carrying amount (EUR 7,892) which remains stable as in 2018 (Raiffeisen Bank International AG 2019b, 65 and 69f.).

5.4.2 Erste Group Bank Aktiengesellschaft

In regard to Erste Group AG, the topics covered for RBI AG, are also considered for this chapter. Consequently, the financial statements are analysed for the financial year 2017 and 2018 as well as for the quarterly report of 2019 (Erste Group Bank AG 2018, 99):

- statement of comprehensive income
- statement of financial position
- statement of financial position according to the measurement categories
- composition of each liability
- breakdown of maturities

The figures are stated in millions of Euro for 2017, 2018 and 2019. With respect to the effective date of IFRS 9, Erste Group AG conducted impact studies. Consequently, the consolidated financial statements 2017 of Erste Group AG state that a part of the portfolio of own bonds issued measured at AC is expected to be categorised into the FVTPL measurement. The carrying amount of own bonds issued measured at AC is EUR 11 billion. As a result, FV changes due to the own credit risk are recorded in the OCI and expected to amount to EUR 0.7 billion of which EUR 0.6 billion is traceable back to new issuances. In terms of the transition regarding equity, it is assumed that a decrease of EUR 0.8 billion before-tax in equity is recognised and further leads to an impact on the accumulated OCI by a loss of EUR 1.1 billion. Moreover, new requirements for the presentation and disclosures are expected with respect to IFRS and FINREP (Erste Group Bank AG 2018, 127f. and 130).

To begin with, the consolidated financial statements of 2017 is analysed. First, the consolidated statement of comprehensive income indicates a disadvantageous development from 2016 to 2017 for items that might not be reclassified to profit or loss from minus EUR 45,227 thousand to minus EUR 640 thousand. This loss is partly offset by the OCI for items that may be reclassified to profit or loss although the amount decreased by EUR 4,664 thousand to EUR 15,030 thousand in 2017. With respect to the consolidated statement of income, the net trading result, the result from financial assets and liabilities designated at FVTPL – for changes in the clean price – as well as gains/losses from financial assets and liabilities not measured at FVTPL (net) – e.g. from derecognition – of Erste Group AG are described. The net trading result remained positive, amounting to EUR 222.8 in 2017. However, the results from financial asset and liabilities designated at FVTPL lead to a loss of EUR 11.5 in 2016 and deteriorated to minus EUR 12.3 in 2017. Considering the results from measurement/repurchase of financial liabilities designated at FVTPL, the loss of EUR 9 in 2016 dropped significantly to minus of EUR 22.6, however, the positive development for financial assets improved the result. For gains/losses from financial assets and liabilities not measured at FVTPL (net) a recovery for repurchases of liabilities measured at AC of EUR 11.2 lead to a gain of EUR 1.3 in 2017 (Erste Group Bank AG 2018, 100f. and 123 and 133f.)

Furthermore, the consolidated statement of changes in equity illustrated no significant outcome on the default risk of Erste Group AG. The total equity and the sub-item retained earning and other reserves increased slightly to EUR 10,542 in 2017 which compromises accumulated net profit on the one side and income/expenses recorded in the OCI on the other side (Erste Group Bank AG 2018, 103 and 161).

With respect to the financial statements 2017, Erste Group AG includes three measurement categories: financial liabilities - held for trading, financial liabilities - at fair value through profit or loss and financial liabilities measured at amortised cost. While the three financial liabilities discussed in the following chapters are included in either FVTPL or AC, financial liabilities held for trading contain derivatives and other trading liabilities which are not described further as no significant impact is described in terms of IFRS 9 (Erste Group Bank AG 2018, 102). With regard to IAS 39, financial liabilities at FVTPL amount to EUR 1,801 (EUR 1,763 in 2016) whereas financial liabilities measured at AC result in EUR 191,711 (EUR 178,909 in 2016) for 2017. In line with IAS 39, the net gains and losses recognised through the P & L amount to negative EUR 23 for the measurement at FVTPL while at AC a gain of EUR 1 in 2017 is illustrated. In contrast, in 2016 the amount for financial liabilities at FVTPL is minus EUR 9 and less than in 2017. For financial liabilities at AC a considerable loss of EUR 12 is shown (Erste Group Bank AG 2018, 233f.). As described in the theoretical part, initial recognition and measurement is consistent within Erste Group AG. However, financial liabilities held for trading include derivatives and other financial liabilities traded excluding hedging instruments. In regard to financial liabilities measured at FVTPL, Erste Group AG aims to reduce accounting mismatches. With the application of the FVO e.g. for portfolios that consist of bonds and funds, FV changes from the own credit risk are booked into the result from financial assets and liabilities designated at FVTPL within the P & L. For the determination of the FV changes due to the change in the own credit risk, Erste

Group AG describes the method in IFRS 7. First, the difference between the present value and market price which is observable at the end is calculated. Second, the sum of the benchmark interest rate at the end and internal rate of return of the instrument at the beginning is required for the calculation of the discount rate (Erste Group Bank AG 2018, 108ff.).

Apart from financial liabilities held for trading and designated at FVTPL, financial liabilities measured at AC also gains and losses from financial assets and liabilities not measured at FVTPL (net) include gains and losses from derecognition, e.g. repurchases. Consequently, the measurement principle is AC whereas the remaining is at FV and at FVTPL (Erste Group Bank AG 2018, 111f.).

In regard to the determination of the FV, Erste Group AG uses market prices if obtainable i.e. for listed securities, derivatives and liquid OTC bonds. Otherwise, it is obliged to apply valuation models for which observable input parameters are obtained. Nevertheless, judgements are made where no market data is accessible. Financial instruments for which the FVO is exercised, Erste Group AG sets the FV for the financial liability that is similar to an asset held. In addition to that, the FV is adapted by the spread related to the own credit risk of Erste Group AG which is determined via buy-back levels of own issuances. In contrast, standard valuation models such as discounted cash flow models or Monte-Carlo-simulations for complex instruments are applied for financial instruments within liquid markets but also data from transactions that are carried out less and extrapolation techniques are used (Erste Group Bank AG 2018, 125 and 222f.). Furthermore, the FV hierarchy and the instruments categorised within each level are described. For level one of the FV hierarchy, Erste Group AG includes financial instruments for which the quoted market price is accessible and due to that frequency, volume and pricing consistency is of relevance. Financial instruments categorised into level one are exchange traded derivatives, shares, government bonds, other bonds and funds traded in an active market. If no active market exists and the market price is unavailable, then observable market data i.e. yield curves, credit spreads and implied volatilities, are obtained and used for valuation models on level two. This approach applies to OTC derivatives, less liquid shares, bonds and funds as well as own issues. Finally, level three of the FV hierarchy includes financial instruments for which neither quoted market prices nor significant data for the valuation models is available. Consequently, assumptions regarding the estimation of parameters are defined. This is of relevance for internally derived credit spreads for which the PD and LGD are used but is also valid for the estimation of the cost of equity within Erste Group AG. The financial instruments categorised into level three are shares, participations, illiquid bonds, own issues and deposits (Erste Group Bank AG 2018, 224).

After describing the consolidated financial statements of 2017, the topics are described for the consolidated financial statements of 2018. Regarding the consolidated statement of comprehensive income, the illustration implies that new items are introduced. Generally, Erste Group AG decided not to restate amounts of 2017 in regard to IFRS 9. Within the category items that may not be reclassified two additional items: FV reserve of equity instruments and own credit risk reserve are introduced. For the items that may be reclassified to profit or loss, following items are newly listed: FV reserve of debt instruments with the sub-items gains/losses during the period, reclassification adjustments and credit loss allowances. Considering the items that may not be reclassified to profit or loss, a considerable improvement from minus EUR 640 thousand to EUR 122,218 thousand for 2018 is shown. However, items that may be reclassified to profit or loss decreased substantially from EUR 15,030 thousand to minus EUR 191,755 in 2018. Regarding the consolidated statement of income, Erste Group AG includes new items which show no comparable figures, for instance other gains/losses from derecognition of financial instruments not measured at FVTPL. However, before the additional item is described, the net trading result is examined. The net trading result dropped from EUR 222,802 thousand to minus EUR 1,697 thousand in 2018 due to the loss in securities and derivatives trading. The gains/losses from financial instruments measured at FVTPL, however, recovered from a loss of EUR 12,302 thousand in 2017 to EUR 195,406 thousand in 2018. One reason for that is the result from measurement/repurchase of financial liabilities designated at FVTPL as the amount substantially increased from minus EUR 22.6 to EUR 154.1 in 2018. It is important to point out, however, that a loss of EUR 13.5 caused by the repurchase of own debt securities issued is booked from the own credit risk reserve into retained earnings. Furthermore, gains/losses from financial assets and liabilities not measured at FVTPL (net) affect solely the asset side. The new item included in the consolidated statement of income is other gains/losses from derecognition of financial instruments not measured at FVTPL which represent the derecognition of financial liabilities at AC resulting in a gain of EUR 9.1 in 2018 (Erste Group Bank AG 2019a, 105f. and 113 and 147 and 149).

While the consolidated statement of changes in equity in 2017 did not show any specific negative outcome, the results for 2018 due to the initial application of IFRS 9 indicate a loss of EUR 734 in terms of the own credit risk reserve as of 1 January 2018. At the end of 2018, the own credit risk reserve recovered slightly, totalling to a loss of EUR 435 which is partly traceable back to the OCI (Erste Group Bank AG 2019a, 109).

With respect to the consolidated balance sheet in 2018, the measurement categories remain as in 2017: financial liabilities held for trading, financial liabilities at fair value through profit or loss and financial liabilities at amortised cost. Financial liabilities at FVTPL increased tremendously from EUR 1,801,245 thousand to EUR 14,121,895 thousand in 2018. Financial liabilities at AC rose from EUR 191,711,402 thousand to a total of EUR 196,862,845 thousand in 2018 (Erste Group Bank AG 2019a, 108). Regarding the transition impact of IFRS 9, the carrying amount in line with IAS 39 is equal to the carrying amount in IFRS 9 for financial liabilities at AC. However, financial liabilities at AC also contain the classification designated at FVTPL as new classification under IFRS 9 which shows an increase in the carrying amount from EUR 12,589 (IAS 39) to EUR 13,031 (IFRS 9) in 2018. Furthermore, financial liabilities at FVTPL are described for deposits from customers and debt securities issued separately as the portfolio affects the FV option (Erste Group Bank AG 2019a, 114f.) In regard to the reconciliation, Erste Group AG uses the measurement categories therefore the illustration of each liability as applied for RBI AG is not possible. However, the reconciliation is described as follows (Erste Group Bank AG 2019a, 117):

in EUR million	IAS 39 Carrying amount 31 Dec 2017	Reclassifications	Remeasurement	IFRS 9 Carrying amount 1 Jan 2018	Retained earnings effects	OCI effects
Amortised cost	192,649	0	0	192,649	0	0
Subtractions: to IFRS 9 FVO (IAS 39: AC)	0	-12,589	0	-12,589	0	0
Total change	0	-12,589	0	-12,589	0	0
Total – AC	192,649	-12,589	0	180,060	0	0

Table 17 | Erste Group AG - Reconciliation amortised cost

(Source: Erste Group Bank AG 2019a, 117)

The AC and the total AC include deposits from customers and banks, debt securities issued as well as other financial liabilities. The loss resulting from the reclassification is due to the previously at AC measured financial liabilities at FVTPL that affect debt securities issued and deposits from customers (Erste Group Bank AG 2019a, 117). In addition to that, the reconciliation of financial liabilities designated at FVTPL are described in the following table (Erste Group Bank AG 2019a, 117):

in EUR million	IAS 39 Carrying amount 31 Dec 2017	Reclassi-fications	Remeasure-ment	IFRS 9 Carrying amount 1 Jan 2018	Retained earnings effects	OCI effects
FVTPL	4,953	0	0	4,953	0	0
Additions:						
From IAS 39 AC	0	12,589	442	13,031	161	-603
From IAS 39 FVO to IFRS 9 FVO (reclassification of FV change due to credit risk)	0	0	0	0	145	-145
From hedge accounting	0	58	0	58	0	0
Total change	0	12,647	442	13,089	306	-748
Total – FVTPL	4,953	12,647	442	18,042	306	-748
Total – financial liabilities	197,602	58	442	198,102	306	-748

Table 18 | Erste Group AG - Reconciliation fair value through profit or loss

(Source: Erste Group Bank AG 2019a, 117f.)

The amount stated in FVTPL of EUR 4,953 and total financial liabilities include derivatives held for trading, other financial liabilities and financial liabilities at FVTPL which contain deposits from customers and debt securities issued. It is important to point out, however, that the amount of EUR 58 is the carrying amount of derivatives intended for hedge accounting derivatives that are reclassified as held for trading (Erste Group Bank AG 2019a, 118f.).

With regard to the measurement of financial instruments, Erste Group AG distinguishes between amortised cost and effective interest rate and fair value. The amortised cost of a financial liability is determined by the effective interest rate. This interest rate is used as discount rate for the estimated future cash payments or receipts for the expected life of a financial liability. In contrast, the FV is determined as described for the consolidated financial statements of 2017 (Erste Group Bank AG 2019a, 121). With IFRS 9, adaptions are conducted for financial liabilities at FVTPL. The category includes financial liabilities designated at FVTPL and financial liabilities held for trading which remains as separate item within the balance sheet. Moreover, Erste Group AG exercises the FVO for the circumstance of an accounting mismatch regarding the measurement at AC. Another relevant aspect is the own credit risk recorded in the OCI and the accumulated OCI assigned to the own credit risk reserve in the statement of changes in equity. Reclassifications to the P & L are not allowed but instead a transfer into retained earnings is possible for financial liabilities derecognised. The credit spread is calculated as the difference between the yield of the financial liability and the interest rate observable at initial recognition. The credit spread set at initial recognition remains for the financial liability, however, the difference between the cumulative amount of the credit risk at the end and beginning is booked into the OCI (Erste Group Bank AG 2019a, 123f.). In regard to the FV of financial liabilities designated at FVTPL, similar assets are considered. Additionally, Erste Group AG considers the principle of market opportunity cost and the cost of the issuance of primary benchmark bonds for the estimation of the own credit spread. In line with the seniority of bonds issued, Erste Group AG uses a specified valuation curve and obtains indications from external investment banks for the determination of the credit spread (Erste Group Bank AG 2019a, 241).

Finally, the interim consolidated financial statements for the first quarter of 2019 is analysed. As in previous consolidated financial statements, the same topics are included for Q1 2019. Beginning with the consolidated statement of comprehensive income, Erste Group AG incurred significant losses compared to Q1 2018 for items that may not be reclassified to profit or loss and items that may be reclassified to profit or loss which resulted in a minus of EUR 31,428 thousand and minus EUR 39,239 thousand in Q1 2019. It is important to point out, however, that the own credit risk reserve is considered as item that may not be reclassified to profit or loss and recovered slightly as the loss of EUR 35,884 thousand in Q1 2018 decreased to minus EUR 25,088 thousand in Q1 2019. Regarding the consolidated statement of income, the net trading result increased substantially from EUR 11,319 thousand in the adjusted quarter one of 2018 to EUR 153,302 thousand for Q1 2019 due to securities and derivatives whereas gains/losses from financial instruments measured at FVTPL decreased from EUR 30,275 thousand to minus EUR 77,107 thousand. The reason for that is the loss of EUR 111 attributable to the result from measurement/repurchase of financial liabilities designated at FVTPL in Q1 2019 which previously showed a gain of EUR 37.4. Another decrease is allocated to other gains/losses from derecognition of financial instruments not measured at FVTPL from EUR 4,094 thousand to EUR 715 thousand in Q1 2019. However, the derecognition of financial liabilities at AC recovered from minus EUR 0.9 in Q1 2018 to minus EUR 0.6 in Q1 2019 (Erste Group Bank AG 2019b, 16f. and 26f.).

In regard to the consolidated statement of changes in equity, Erste Group AG managed to improve the own credit risk reserve as part of the OCI. While it amounts to minus EUR 25 for the beginning of 2018, the loss is EUR 15 for 1 January 2019 (Erste Group Bank AG 2019b, 20).

Within the consolidated balance sheet, both measurement categories indicate an increase from December 2018 to March 2019. While financial liabilities at FVTPL increased from EUR 14,121,895 thousand to EUR 14,449,035 in Q1 2019, financial liabilities at AC rose slightly higher from EUR 196,862,845 thousand to

EUR 201,356,979 thousand (Erste Group Bank AG 2019b, 19). Regarding the FV measurement and hierarchy, no changes are described in Q1 2019 (Erste Group Bank AG 2019b, 61).

5.4.2.1 Deposits from customers

Starting with the consolidated financial statements 2017, deposits from customers are listed within the consolidated balance sheet in line with the measurement categories. Consequently, deposits from customers are set as financial liability – at fair value through profit or loss and as financial liability measured at amortised cost. Deposits from customers measured at FVTPL decreased from EUR 73,917 thousand in 2016 to EUR 48,559 thousand in 2017, whereas the measurement at AC increased significantly from EUR 137,938,808 thousand in 2016 to EUR 150,920,715 thousand in 2017. From this point of view, the majority is measured at AC (Erste Group Bank AG 2018, 102).

Considering the measurement at FVTPL, the figures previously stated are the carrying amounts and did not change in comparison to the amount repayable. Furthermore, the FV changes that are due to the own credit risk showed a negative EUR 0.1 in 2016 but lead to a positive EUR 0.1 in the cumulative amount. In contrast, deposits from customers indicate no effect on FV changes but include EUR 0.1 in the cumulative amount in 2017 (Erste Group Bank AG 2018, 154).

With respect to the measurement at AC, deposits from customers are divided into overnight deposits (EUR 85,707 in 2016 and EUR 99,278 in 2017), term deposits that decreased by EUR 1,5 to EUR 50,576 in 2017 and repurchase agreements that rose significantly from EUR 156 in 2016 to EUR 1,066 in 2017. These sub-items are further split into positions (Erste Group Bank AG 2018, 155).

Another point to consider is the FV hierarchy for deposits from customers. It is important to point out, however, that only at FV measured financial instruments are relevant. While the FV of deposits from customers measured at FVTPL is higher in 2016, a decrease of EUR 25 million resulted in a total of EUR 49 in 2017 which is categorised into level two of the FV hierarchy. Additionally, the FV is presented for deposits from customers that are measured at AC. The carrying amount increased by EUR 12,982 to EUR 150,921 and the FV rose by EUR 13,003 to EUR 151,168 in 2017. The carrying amount is slightly below the FV in 2016 and 2017 and is solely allocated to level three. For the calculation, Erste Group AG considers the current interest rate and its own credit spreads (Erste Group Bank AG 2018, 225 and 231).

Regarding the remaining maturities, deposits from customers measured at FVTPL are categorised below one year in 2016 and 2017 whereas for the measurement at AC, amounts below and above one year are assigned. Nevertheless, the amount for a remaining maturity of below one year is significantly higher leading to EUR 109,847 for below one year and EUR 41,074 for a maturity above one year (Erste Group Bank AG 2018, 237).

With respect to the consolidated financial statements 2018, deposits from customers measured at FVTPL increased significantly from EUR 48,559 thousand to EUR 211,810 thousand. In contrast, deposits from customers measured at AC rose from EUR 150,920,715 thousand to EUR 162,426,423 thousand for 2018 (Erste Group Bank AG 2019a, 108).

With respect to deposits categorised as financial liabilities at FVTPL, the carrying amount increased significantly from EUR 49 to EUR 212 in 2018 and the amount repayable increased from EUR 49 to EUR 194 in 2018. In terms of the FV changes resulting from the own credit risk, the amount of minus EUR 1 is recognised while the cumulative amount is EUR 4 in 2018. For the measurement at AC, overnight deposits contributed to the increase as it rose by EUR 10,923 to EUR 110,201 in 2018 whereas term deposits remained constant at EUR 50,743 and repurchase agreements rose slightly to EUR 1,483 in 2018. Deposits from customers within the FV hierarchy increased from EUR 49 to EUR 212 in 2018 remaining in level two of the FV hierarchy. Financial instruments for which the FV is not measured, deposits from customers showed an increase in the carrying amount and consequently in the FV traceable back to level three. The carrying amount of EUR 162,426 exceeds the FV of EUR 162,179 in 2018 (Erste Group Bank AG 2019a, 170f. and 243 and 248).

Regarding the transition impact of IFRS 9, financial liabilities at FVTPL regarding deposits from customers indicate no effect on the carrying amount using IAS 39 and IFRS 9. It is reasonable to assume that these financial liabilities belong to the FV option portfolio (Erste Group Bank AG 2019a, 114). Additionally, Erste Group AG conducted de-designations that lead to designations from financial liabilities measured at AC in line with IAS 39 to financial liabilities designated at FVTPL. This designation resulted in an increase of the carrying amount in line with IAS 39 as of 31 December 2017 from EUR 48 to a total of EUR 186 in line with IFRS 9 for 1 January 2018. The reclassification amounts to EUR 133 whereas the remeasurement lead to EUR 4 (Erste Group Bank AG 2019a, 120).

For the remaining maturities in the consolidated financial statements 2018, deposits from customers that used to be classified below one year in 2017, are split into both maturities, however, the remaining maturity above one year amounts to EUR 137 while those below one year amount to EUR 75 in 2018. Contrarily, deposits from customers measured at AC show an increase in deposits below one year and a decrease above one year resulting in EUR 132,406 and EUR 30,021 in 2018 respectively (Erste Group Bank AG 2019a, 253).

With respect to the interim consolidated financial statements of Q1 2019, Erste Group AG shows an increase within deposits from customers measured at FVTPL by EUR 17,036 thousand to EUR 228,846 thousand in Q1 2019. Moreover, deposits from customer measured at AC rose slightly to EUR 165,555,646 thousand in Q1 mainly attributable to term deposits (Erste Group Bank AG 2019b, 19 and 35). Considering the FV hierarchy, deposits from customers measured at FVTPL remain within level two but increased from EUR 212 at the end of 2018 to EUR 229 in Q1 2019. For deposits from customers, the FV is determined although the measurement is not at FV. The carrying amount and FV increased to EUR 165,556 and EUR 165,394, respectively (Erste Group Bank AG 2019b, 63 and 68).

5.4.2.2   Deposits from banks

With regard to the consolidated financial statements 2017, deposits from banks are categorised as deposits from customers. It is important to point out, however, that deposits from banks categorised into FVTPL show a result of zero for 2016 and 2017. Considering the carrying amount and amount repayable, the figure also remains zero for both years. Additionally, FV changes are not assigned due to changes in the own credit risk of Erste Group AG. However, deposits from banks measured at AC indicate an increase of EUR 1,718,029 thousand leading to an amount of EUR 16,349,382 thousand in 2017 (Erste Group Bank AG 2018, 102 and 154). Regarding the measurement at AC, the items that are listed within deposits from banks are overnight deposits that decreased from EUR 3,557 to EUR 3,460 in 2017, term deposits that slightly increased to EUR 11,893 in 2017 and repurchase agreements that decreased from EUR 1,534 in 2016 to EUR 996 in 2017 (Erste Group Bank AG 2018, 155). With respect to the FV hierarchy, deposits from banks are neither listed in 2016 nor 2017. Nevertheless, deposits from banks are illustrated in the table of financial instruments not measured at FV considering the carrying amount and FV. The carrying amount and FV in 2016 increased to EUR 16,349 and EUR 16,421 respectively in 2017. Moreover, the carrying amount in 2016 is slightly higher than the FV whereas it is reversely for 2017. In regard to the allocation of the FV, deposits from banks are solely categorised into level three of the FV hierarchy. As with deposits from customers, the FV of deposits from banks allocated into level three is derived from the current interest rate and own credit spread (Erste Group Bank AG 2018, 225 and 231).

Another point to consider is the allocation of deposits from banks in terms of remaining maturities. Deposits from banks show a result of zero for 2016 and 2017 regarding the measurement at FVTPL below and above one year. In contrast to that, deposits from banks measured at AC are higher for remaining maturities below one year similar to deposits from customers. However, the amount is significantly lower than for deposits from customers. The amount of EUR 10,871 is set for the term below one year whereas EUR 5,478 is assigned to remaining maturities above one year (Erste Group Bank AG 2018, 237).

With respect to the consolidated financial statements of 2018, deposits from banks measured at AC increased slightly from EUR 16,349,382 thousand to EUR 17,657,544 thousand in 2018 which results from the increase in overnight deposits and repurchase agreements. As deposits from banks are not designated at FVTPL, neither the FV nor the change in the own credit risk is required (Erste Group Bank AG 2019a, 108 and 170f.). For deposits from banks not measured at FV, the disclosures illustrate a slight increase to EUR 17,658 and EUR 17,752 in the carrying among and FV, respectively for 2018 attributable to level three (Erste Group Bank AG 2019a, 248). With regard to the remaining maturities, deposits from banks are listed solely within financial liabilities at AC indicating a slight increase for below and above one year leading to EUR 11,915 and EUR 5,743 in 2018 (Erste Group Bank AG 2019a, 253).

The interim consolidated financial statements for Q1 2019 indicate that deposits from banks measured at AC rose by EUR 2,637 to EUR 20,295 in Q1 2019 (Erste Group Bank AG 2019b, 35). For deposits from banks, the carrying amount and FV increased in regard to financial instruments not measured at FV. While the carrying amount and FV amount to EUR 17,658 and EUR 17,752 respectively at the end of 2018, both amounts increased to EUR 20,295 and EUR 20,464 in Q1 2019. Consequently, the FV amount exceeds the carrying amount in both years (Erste Group Bank AG 2019b, 68).

5.4.2.3   Own issuance

The financial statements of 2017 indicate the measurement categories as for deposits from customers and banks. Therefore, debt securities issued are measured at FVTPL and remain relatively stable leading to a result of EUR 1,752,686 thousand in 2017. In contrast to that, debt securities issued for which the AC measurement is chosen, the amount of EUR 23,342,123 thousand in 2017 showed a decrease of EUR 2,160,498 thousand (Erste Group Bank AG 2018, 102).

For debt securities issued measured at FVTPL, the carrying amount of EUR 1,753 in 2017 represents the highest proportion compared to deposits from customers and banks. However, the carrying amount of debt securities issued in 2017 differed from the amount repayable which amounts to EUR 1,668 in 2017. Consequently, the difference amounts to EUR 85 in 2017. Additionally, debt securities issued measured at FVTPL account for the highest FV changes due to the own credit risk of Erste Group AG. While the FV change amounts to EUR 18.2 in 2016, the amount increased significantly to EUR 90.9 in 2017. For the same reason, the cumulative amount showed an increase from EUR 57 to EUR 145.7 in 2017. Considering the items that lead to the total amount of debt securities issued measured at FVTPL, subordinated liabilities increased by EUR 324 to EUR 880 in 2017 whereas debt securities issued decreased from EUR 1,133 in 2016 to a total of EUR 873 in the reporting year 2017. In contrast, the items that are categorised within debt securities issued measured at AC, decreased slightly. Therefore, subordinated liabilities amount to EUR 4,937 and other debt securities issued fell to EUR 18,405 in 2017 (Erste Group Bank AG 2018, 154).

Within the FV hierarchy, financial liabilities at FVTPL include deposits from customers and debt securities issued. For the reporting year 2017, a slight increase is shown. While level two amounts to EUR 1,599 in 2016, EUR 1,753 is set for 2017. However, financial instruments categorised into level three amount to EUR 90 in 2016 but for 2017 indicated no FV result. Furthermore, the FV is illustrated for debt securities issued measured at AC. The carrying amount and FV decreased from 2016 to 2017 to EUR 23,342 and EUR 24,876 in the reporting year. Nevertheless, in both years the FV exceeds the carrying amount. The allocation to the levels remained relatively stable from 2016 to 2017. The majority is attributable to level two with EUR 22,282, followed by level one amounting to EUR 1,780 and level three indicating EUR 814 in 2017. The FV is derived by market prices, observable market data or discounted future cash flows adapted by the own credit risk through buy-back levels of own issuances (Erste Group Bank AG 2018, 225 and 231).

With regards to the remaining maturities, debt securities issued measured at FVTPL contain the highest proportion for remaining maturities above one year and remain constant to the previous year. The amount for below one year is EUR 224 while above one year results in EUR 1,529 in 2017. Compared to that, the amounts decreased slightly from 2016 to 2017 for debt securities issued measured at AC resulting in EUR 2,928 and EUR 20,415 in 2017 respectively for below and above one year (Erste Group Bank AG 2018, 237).

For the consolidated financial statements 2018, debt securities issued measured at FVTPL increased substantially from EUR 1,752,686 thousand to EUR 13,445,678 thousand in 2018 whereas the measurement at AC lead to a decrease from EUR 23,342,123 thousand to EUR 16,292,610 thousand in 2018 (Erste Group Bank AG 2019a, 108). Considering the measurement at FVTPL, the carrying amount and the amount repayable increased substantially to EUR 13,446 and EUR 12,706 that lead to a difference of EUR 740 in 2018 while in 2017 the difference solely amounts to EUR 85. It is important to point out, however, that FV changes of the own credit risk of debt securities issued dropped considerably. The FV changes amount to EUR 91 in 2017 and fell to minus EUR 226 in 2018. Nevertheless, the cumulative amount increased from EUR 146 to EUR 502 in 2018. In regard to the items that are included within debt securities issued, significant increases are shown for each item e.g. subordinated debt securities issued increased from EUR 880 to EUR 4.879 in 2018 and other debt securities issued increased from EUR 873 to EUR 8.567 in 2018 which is contributed to bonds with an increase from EUR 502 to EUR 5.469 in 2018. Considering debt securities issued measured at AC, the amounts decreased e.g. subordinated debt securities issued fell from EUR 4,937 to EUR 951 in 2018, other debt securities issued decreased from EUR 18,405 to EUR 15,341 in 2018 of which the sub-item bonds indicated a decrease from EUR 8,474 to EUR 3,073 in the reporting year. In regard to the FV hierarchy and the FV levels, debt securities issued changed. While in 2017, solely level two (EUR 1,753) is affected, each level is used for the FV determination in 2018. Level one amounts to EUR 618, level two increased significantly to EUR 12,731 due to the reclassification from AC and level three totalled to EUR 96 in 2018. For debt securities issued but not measured at FV, the carrying amount and FV decreased to EUR 16,293 and EUR 16,478 respectively in 2018. Considering each level, level one rose significantly from EUR 1,780 to EUR 6,761 in 2018, level two decreased from EUR 22,282 to EUR 9,544 in 2018 and level three also fell from EUR 814 to EUR 172 in the reporting year (Erste Group Bank AG 2019a, 170f. and 243 and 248).

Considering the transition impact, debt securities issued and deposits from customers measured at FVTPL indicate no difference in the carrying amount for IAS 39 and IFRS 9 as at 1 January 2018. Additionally, debt securities issued measured at FVTPL are categorised into the FV option portfolio (Erste Group Bank AG 2019a, 114). As for deposits from customers, also debt securities issued are considered for the designation of existing financial liabilities as measured at FVTPL due to IFRS 9. The main reason for the designation is based on the elimination of the accounting mismatch as derivatives are used for hedging. The results regarding the transition are shown in the table below (Erste Group Bank AG 2019a, 120):

in EUR million	IAS 39 Carrying amount 31 Dec 17	Reclassifi-cation	Remeasure-ment	IFRS 9 Carrying amount 1 Jan 2018
Financial liabilities designated at FVTPL – debt securities issued	1,753	11,922	437	14,112
From IAS 39 financial liabilities – held for trading/Derivatives		270		270
From IAS 39 financial assets – held for trading/Derivatives		-26		-26
From IAS 39 financial liabilities at AC – debt securities issued		11,143	437	11,580
From IAS 39 changes in FV in portfolio hedged items		509		509
From IAS 39 other liabilities		27		27

Table 19 | Erste Group AG - De-designation upon transition to IFRS 9

(Source: Erste Group Bank AG 2019a, 120)

For the remaining maturities of debt securities issued significant increases are recognised within the measurement at FVTPL – from EUR 224 to EUR 1,197 for below one year and EUR 1,529 to EUR 12,249 for above one year in 2018. For the measurement at AC, the remaining maturity below one year increased to

EUR 4,312 whereas a reduction in the amount for above one year is recognised amounting to EUR 11,981 in 2018 (Erste Group Bank AG 2019a, 253).

Finally, the interim consolidated financial statements of Q1 2019 illustrated an increase for debt securities issued measured at FVTPL as most sub-items such as subordinated debt securities or bonds rose, thereby leading to a total of EUR 13,784. Nevertheless, debt securities issued measured at AC decreased from EUR 16,293 to EUR 14,886 in Q1 2019 due to the decrease in other debt securities issued (Erste Group Bank AG 2019b, 35f.). For the FV hierarchy, debt securities issued measured at FVTPL show increases in the three levels, however, level two accounts for the majority with EUR 13,028 and totals to EUR 13,784. In contrast, the FV of debt securities issued not measured at FVTPL, the carrying amount and FV decreased slightly from 2018 to Q1 2019. Therefore, the carrying amount is EUR 14,886 whereas the FV amounts to EUR 15,141 (Erste Group Bank AG 2019b, 63 and 68).

5.5 Summary of the main differences between RBI AG and Erste Group AG

The findings of the empirical analysis in chapter 5.4 of RBI AG and Erste Group AG are briefly summarised and compared to each other. For this reason, no additional references are used in this chapter. Generally, relevant topics for each consolidated financial statements are described for 2017, 2018 and Q1 2019.

To begin with, RBI AG illustrated in the consolidated financial statements 2017 the merge with Raiffeisen Zentralbank Österreich AG and applied IFRS 9.7.1.2 regarding the presentation of financial liabilities measured at FVTPL. In contrast to that, Erste Group AG did not conduct new standards prior to the date of effectiveness. For 2018, RBI AG applied the new standards of IFRS 9 and set the reporting in line with the FINREP. Consequently, RBI AG and Erste Group AG did not adapt comparative information related to classification and measurement changes.

In regard to the statement other comprehensive income and total comprehensive income, RBI AG incurred a loss of EUR 139,643 thousand due to FV changes attributable to the default risk of RBI AG. Due to the significant loss, the cumulative change for the FVO within retained earnings showed a negative EUR 64,052 thousand in 2017. For the consolidated financial statements 2018, FV changes due to the default risk of RBI AG improved from minus EUR 139,064 thousand to EUR 33,692 thousand. Applying IFRS 9, RBI AG decided to reclassify financial liabilities designated at FV to the measurement at AC leading to a carrying amount of EUR 447,781 thousand. It is important to point out that the reclassification resulted in a substantial decrease in the FV due to the default risk of RBI AG. The difference between the FV of liabilities opting in for the FVO and the amount contractually to be paid amounts to EUR 597,508 thousand in 2017. However, the result amounted to minus EUR 404,000 thousand which is attributable to the reclassification from FV to AC in 2018. This amount decreased further to minus EUR 406 million in Q1 2019.

With regard to the comprehensive income of Erste Group AG in the consolidated financial statements 2017, the amendments of IFRS 9 are not considered prior to the official date. Consequently, a considerable loss is incurred in 2017. Nevertheless, the comprehensive income is adapted in 2018 leading to the introduction of the FV reserve of equity instruments indicating a loss of EUR 152,264 thousand and an own credit risk reserve representing a positive figure. The interim consolidated financial statements Q1 2019 illustrated a loss for the consolidated statement of comprehensive income whereas the credit risk reserve improved partly.

The income statement of RBI AG in 2017 shows the net income from derivatives and liabilities to which the net income from liabilities designated at FV is categorised. While a net income is realised in 2017, the comparable figure in 2016 reflects the movements in market interest rates as well as the default risk of RBI AG which is below the figure in 2017 (EUR 119,064 thousand). For the consolidated financial statements 2018, the net income is considered as net trading income and FV result in line with the measurement e.g. held for trading and designated at FVTPL. While the relevant financial liabilities at held for trading incurred losses, the measurement at FVTPL remained stable. In regard to the derecognition of financial liabilities, losses incurred for deposits and other financial liabilities in 2017 while no amount is shown in 2018. However, the derecognition of debt securities issued deteriorated from 2017 to 2018. For the interim consolidated financial statements of Q1 2019, RBI AG indicated a loss for deposits held for trading and designated at FVTPL. Additionally, debt securities issued showed a loss measured at FVTPL. Nevertheless, FV changes due to the credit risk of RBI AG improved to EUR 4 million in 2019.

In regard to the consolidated financial statements 2017, Erste Group AG managed to achieve a net trading result although losses from financial assts and liabilities designated at FVTPL occured. Moreover, the net trading result is influenced by losses in the measurement/repurchase of financial liabilities designated at FVTPL whereas gains/losses from financial assets and liabilities not measured at FVTPL contributed to an improvement. The statement of income in 2018 included another new position – other gains/losses from derecognition of financial instruments not measured at FVTPL which indicate a gain. However, the net trading result indicated a considerable drop. While gains/losses from financial instruments measured at FVTPL recovered, the measurement/repurchase of financial liabilities designated at FVTPL dropped significantly. The net trading result increased for Q1 2019 whereas the remaining items e.g. gains/losses from financial instruments measured at FVTPL or the result from measurement/repurchase of financial liabilities designated at FVTPL decreased.

With respect to the changes in equity of RBI AG in 2018, the unrealised net gain of EUR 33,692 thousand due to the reclassification is shown, however, IFRS 9 lead to a decrease in equity amounting to minus EUR 169,438 thousand of which EUR 69,938 are accounted for previously at FV designated deposits and debt instruments. In Q1 2019, the changes in equity affect retained earnings and the cumulative OCI leading to a positive result.

For the consolidated financial statements of Erste Group AG in 2017, the statement of changes in equity represented a slight increase in retained earning and other reserves whereas the results in 2018 showed a loss of EUR 734 million as a consequence of IFRS 9 and the own credit risk reserve. For Q1 2019, the change in the own credit risk reserve, part of the changes in equity, improved although the loss amounts to EUR 25,088 thousand.

The FV measurement and FV hierarchy in 2017, 2018 and Q1 2019 are equal to the theoretical part. Within level one RBI AG includes listed securities, derivatives and liquid bonds on the OTC market, in level two are OTC-derivatives and non-quoted debt instruments and level three contains credit spreads derived from internal estimates. However, most financial liabilities are measured at AC thereby requiring the effective interest rate method.

The procedure is similar to the consolidated financial statements of Erste Group AG. Financial instruments assigned to level one is for instance exchange traded derivatives, shares or government bonds. Level two contains OTC-derivatives, bonds and own issues whereas level three includes credit spreads relevant for illiquid bonds, own issues and deposits. However, within the consolidated financial statements 2017, for financial liabilities measured at FVTPL thereby applying the FVO, the calculation of the own credit risk is obtained from IFRS 7.

Regarding the consolidated financial statements of RBI AG in 2018, the financial positions are adapted in line with IFRS 9. While in 2017 each liability is illustrated separately, the following measurement categories are shown: financial liabilities – AC, financial liabilities – designated at FVTPL and financial liabilities – held for trading. Therefore, the transition is presented in accordance with the measurement categories. While initially the objective of the examination is to determine the consequences of moving from AC to FV, RBI AG instead reclassified financial liabilities at FVTPL to AC. As a result, the carrying amount increased for financial liabilities measured at AC for 1 January 2018 while financial liabilities measured at FVTPL decreased due to reclassification and remeasurements. The effect of IFRS 9 on equity is solely attributable to remeasurements.

With respect to the financial positions and measurement categories, Erste Group AG considers as RBI AG three measurement categories in the consolidated financial statements of 2017. As a result, net gains and losses are recognised in line with the measurement category. Therefore, the measurement at FVTPL lead to a loss in the P & L while the measurement at AC resulted in a gain.

With respect to the financial liabilities of RBI AG, deposits from customers are described for 2017, 2018 and Q1 2019. The consolidated financial statements 2018 showed the reclassification of deposits from customers designated at FVTPL dated 1 January 2017. Therefore, the measurement at AC increased whereas the amount of deposits from customers measured at FVTPL is set at zero at 31 December 2017. In regard to the consolidated financial statements 2018, the carrying amount of deposits from customers applying IAS 39 amounts to EUR 616,867 thousand (31 December 2017) and decreased to EUR 530,796 thousand due to reclassifications and remeasurements of IFRS 9 (1 January 2018). The effect on retained earnings amounts to EUR 12,445 thousand whereas the cumulative OCI showed EUR 2,826 thousand in 2018. In Q1 2019 no significant impact is illustrated. For deposits from banks, the reconciliation showed solely the measurement at AC for the beginning of 2017 whereas the measurement at AC decreased to EUR 21,674,563 thousand and a reclassification lead to the measurement at FVTPL of EUR 616,867 thousand at the end of 2017. As only a relatively small proportion is measured at FVTPL, no further impact due to IFRS 9 is described for deposits from banks. Finally, within the reconciliation of the consolidated financial statements 2018, debt securities issued by RBI AG decreased slightly. The measurement at AC decreased from EUR 7,153,963 thousand at 1 January 2017 to EUR 4,765,327 thousand at the end of 2017. In addition, debt securities issued measured at AC illustrated a reduction from EUR 1,373,418 thousand for the beginning of 2017 to EUR 1,119,810 at the end of the year. In regard to the transition for 2018, the carrying amount of debt securities issued in line with IAS 39 decreased from EUR 1,891,754 thousand to a carrying amount of EUR 1,460,107 thousand in line with IFRS 9. While additions of at AC measured financial liabilities in reclassification and remeasurements contributed to a slight increase, the subtraction of financial liabilities at AC contributed to the considerable decrease. Apart from that, additions lead to a negative EUR 104 thousand whereas subtractions accounted for minus EUR 2,089 thousand in retained earnings. A positive effect is traceable back to subtractions due to EUR 56,860 thousand in the cumulative OCI.

In regard to the consolidated financial statements 2018, Erste Group AG presented the transition impact of IFRS 9 in line with the measurement categories instead of showing the impact for each liability. For the reconciliation of financial liabilities measured at AC, Erste Group AG indicates a decrease in the carrying amount between IAS 39 amounting to EUR 192,649 million and IFRS 9 resulting in EU 180,060 million. The difference is traceable back to reclassifications regarding the FVO which neither effects retained earnings nor OCI. For the reconciliation of financial liabilities designated at FVTPL, additions from the reclassifications and remeasurement of at AC measured financial liabilities are assigned. Moreover, the FV change caused by the own default risk is recognised as a gain of EUR 145 million in retained earnings. However, the movement from IAS 39 to IFRS 9 resulted in a negative OCI effect of minus EUR

145 million. Nevertheless, the reconciliation of financial liabilities at FVTPL lead to an increase in the carrying amount of IFRS 9 with a total of EUR 198,102 million. With respect to the liabilities of Erste Group AG, deposits from customers showed no effect in the OCI due to the own default risk in 2017 while a loss of EUR 1 million is recognised in 2018. The transition impact of IFRS 9 in 2018 lead to an increase of the carrying amount because of the measurement applying IAS 39 and IFRS 9 respectively. The carrying amount increased through reclassifications and remeasurement from EUR 48 million to EUR 186 million using IFRS 9. For deposits from banks, measurement is only conducted at AC, thereby indicating no significant effects due to IFRS 9.

Finally, debt securities issued by Erste Group AG showed within the consolidated financial statements 2017, the highest FV changes due to the own credit risk amounting to EUR 90.9 million which dropped significantly to a loss of EUR 226 million in 2018. The transition impact of IFRS 9 lead to significant increase in debt securities issued measured at FVTPL. The main driver is the reclassification amounting to EUR 11,143 million and remeasurement of EUR 437 million of financial liabilities measured at AC. Applying IFRS 9, the carrying amount rose from EUR 1,753 million to EUR 14,112 million.

6 Conclusion

The conclusion of this paper describes the theory and empirical analysis which is further necessary in order to answer the central question of this paper regarding the impact of IFRS 9 in terms of liabilities. Further, it is examined whether the FVO is exercised leading to the change from AC to FV as IFRS 9 is effective since 1 January 2018. The reason for the amendments of IFRS 9 are traceable back to the measurement of the credit spread. During the financial crisis, the creditworthiness deteriorated and financial institutions recognised the increase in the credit spread in the P & L as earning whereas the FV of the financial liability decreased. Consequently, this approach leads to volatility in the P & L. With regards to the objective of the examination, this paper examines three banking products – deposits from customers, deposits from banks and debt securities issued – from a theoretical point of view and a comparison of consolidated financial statements of RBI AG and Erste Group AG. In order to determine whether IFRS 9 impacts these financial liabilities, the statements are used from the financial years 2017, 2018 and the first quarter of 2019.

With respect to the theoretical part of IFRS 9, the principles of the International Financial Reporting Standards, the main amendments and phases as well as the valuation, classification and measurement under IAS 39 and IFRS 9 for financial assets and liabilities is summarised. Additionally, aspects of the balance sheet and P & L are illustrated whereas banking products on the liability side are described from a theoretical point of view in order to conduct the empirical analysis.

The aim of the principles of the International Financial Reporting Standards Framework stated in IAS 1, is to set consistent standards applying IFRS. Principles include e.g. the fair presentation and compliance with IFRS, the going concern principle relevant for the future development, the frequency of reporting and the requirement to illustrate comparative information regarding the presentation of financial statements. The second topic described are the main amendments within the phases of IFRS 9 which is essential due to the length of each project. Beginning with phase one, the main topic covers classification and measurement for financial assets and liabilities. The classification of financial assets is set in line with the business model and the contractual cash flows introduced. Thereby the evaluation depends on an objective set for a group of financial assets and is further determined by contractual cash flow which determines whether a financial asset is held, sold or held and sold in order to generate cash flows. Moreover, the classification categories changed into financial assets at AC, at FVTPL or at FVOCI. Generally, the measurement is conducted at AC unless the conditions defined for the business model and contractual cash flows are met leading to the measurement at FVTPL. The measurement at FVOCI is executed if the business model states that contractual cash flows are obtained from holding and selling financial assets. However, the measurement is conducted at FV if an accounting mismatch exists, thereby applying the FVO. Moreover, the switch to the measurement at FVOCI is permitted for equity instruments as the contractual cash flow condition is not met. In regard to phase one, the changes for financial liabilities are significantly lower and most parts of IAS 39 remain valid. Therefore, measurement is conducted at either AC or FVTPL unless the financial liability is listed within the exceptions measured at FVTPL e.g. financial liabilities for which the FVO is exercised. The standards for exercising the FVO remain as in IAS 39 for financial liabilities. Therefore, financial liabilities may be grouped in line with the risk or investment strategy. With regards to the treatment of embedded derivatives, IAS 39 prescribes the separation e.g. no linkage between the economic characteristics, which leads to the measurement at AC for the host contract whereas the embedded derivative is measured at FVTPL. The main amendment for financial liabilities affects the treatment of the own credit risk in case the FVO is exercised. In order to avoid the positive effect in the P & L due to the credit risk that initially is caused by a deterioration in the credit risk, the IASB decided that FV changes due to the own credit risk are recorded in the OCI whereas other changes such as effects on the reference interest rates are recognised in the P & L. It is important to point out, however, that changes booked into the OCI are not transferred into the P & L but rather reclassified into equity under accumulated OCI. The credit spread is determined by applying the standard approach which aims to identify the credit spread for the financial instrument which is derived by the difference between the fair value and present value of a financial instrument including the return and reference interest rate. Finally, phase one affects financial assets and liabilities in terms of more demanding reporting duties. Phase two affects amortised cost and impairments for financial assets. As a result, IAS 39 prescribed the usage of the incurred loss model whereas IFRS 9 sets the expected credit loss model implying a three-stage model. The final phase three deals with hedge accounting and the aim to connect hedge accounting to the risk strategy. Further, a financial liability which is recorded in the OCI due to the own credit risk is not permitted to be used as hedge instrument.

As described in phase one, financial assets are impacted by more changes than financial liabilities. In regard to the valuation, classification and measurement under IFRS 9 and IAS 39 the initial recognition is the same for financial assets and liabilities. The asset or liability is recognised if it becomes part of a contractual agreement recorded at initial recognition with the FV. Additionally, the derecognition remains for financial assets and liabilities as stated in IAS 39. While financial assets require a multilevel process of three steps (economical approach, risk and reward approach and control concept) to evaluate whether the right of receiving cash flows expired, financial liabilities or a part of the financial liability are derecognised at repayment, cancellation or expiration of the contract. Moreover, debt instruments bought back by the issuer lead to derecognition and changes are recorded in the P & L. In contrast to that, if a financial liability is repaid or the debtor is legally released, the difference between the carrying amount and actual amount paid are recorded in the P & L for the derecognition. Another circumstance that leads to the derecognition of financial assets and liabilities are substantial modifications. Consequently, the financial instrument is derecognised and re-recognised including the modifications. For financial liabilities, a substantial modification occurs if changes in the present value amount to 10 %.

As illustrated in phase one, the categories for financial assets changed whereas financial liabilities are categorised as in line with IAS 39. Financial assets are categorised in line with the business model – hold to collect, hold to sell or neither hold to collect nor hold to sell – and the contractual cash flows, also referred to as the SPPI-criterion. Financial assets compromise debt instruments, derivatives and equity instruments. The measurement at AC is conducted if the business model is hold to collect and the SPPI-criterion is met. Consequently, disagio/agio and the consideration of the expected loss is booked into the P & L. However, if the business model is hold to sell, the financial asset is measured irrevocably at FVOCI (mandatory), thereby changes in the FV are recorded in the OCI while other changes are recorded in the P & L. The measurement of equity instruments is irrevocably at FVOCI (designated) without recycling. Therefore, all changes are recognised in the OCI except for disagio/agio. However, if the equity instrument is held for trading, the measurement is at FVTPL. Further, the measurement at FVTPL occurs also if neither the business model nor the SPPI-criterion are met or if the FVO is exercised due to an accounting mismatch for debt instruments. In contrast, derivatives are measured at FVTPL for which all changes are booked into the P & L. Reclassifications of financial assets are permitted, however, the conditions must be considered as significant and influencing.

Regarding the categories of financial liabilities, fewer changes are conducted than for assets. Consequently, the categorisation of IAS 39 is equal to IFRS 9. Therefore, financial liabilities are categorised at AC unless the financial liability is listed within the exceptions to be measured at FVTPL e.g. financial guarantees or derivatives with a negative market value. However, it is distinguished between the FVTPL designated and FVTPL held for trading. The main difference is the treatment of the change in the FV due to the own credit risk. While this change is booked into the OCI for FVTPL designated, FVTPL held for trading records those changes in the P & L. Apart from that, the initial recognition and measurement at FV, disagio/agio and other changes in the FV booked into the P & L remain the same for both FVTPL (designated) and FVTPL (mandatory). In contrast, the measurement at AC includes the transaction costs at initial recognition and affects the P & L solely through disagio/agio. As for financial assets, also financial liabilities are permitted to be exercised as FVO if the requirements are met e.g. an accounting mismatch between asset and liability or the measurement at FV in line with the risk management strategy. However, if the FVO exercised leads to an accounting mismatch allocated to the recording in the OCI and P & L, FV changes due to the own credit risk and other FV changes are permitted to be booked solely in the P & L due to the fact that changes in the FV might be offset by changes in the P & L.

With respect to the balance sheet and P & L, the main aspects are described. Beginning with ALM, one task is to manage interest rate and liquidity risk on an aggregated level for the business lines within the bank whereas the risk management is responsible for e.g. the capital regulation and the management of risks on and off the balance sheet. In regard to the P & L, it presents the performance over a given time and consists of revenues and expenses, however, the objective to achieve a net interest income as bank depends on the net yield and the cost of funding. The P & L required additional positions due to the new classification categories in line with IFRS 9 for financial assets e.g. the result of other financial instruments mandatorily measured at FV. Apart from that, changes in the reserve from assessing the own credit risk for financial liabilities do not affect the P & L. In contrast to the P & L, the balance sheet presents assets and liabilities as a snapshot in time. Considering IFRS 9, the main adaptions are carried out for the asset side whereas liabilities remain unchanged to IAS 39.

The final part of the theory, which is relevant for the empirical analysis, is the summary of the banking products. Beginning with deposits from customers, there are sub-items which are similarly to the empirical analysis. Furthermore, the short-term availability of deposits from customers due to withdrawals is also shown in the empirical analysis in regard to the remaining maturities. The main influencing and impacting factors are the maturity transformation and the arising liquidity risk as well as the interest rate risk. Generally, the prerequisite for the initial recognition is based on a contractual agreement. In line with IAS 39, deposits from customers are measured at AC and initially recorded at the FV including the transaction costs. The measurement at AC is conducted through the effective interest rate method. The aim is to determine the effective interest rate which evolves from the difference between the amount paid and the amount repayable. Applying IAS 39, solely disagios/agios and results from derecognitions are recorded in the P & L. Assuming that the FVO is exercised for deposits from customers, every FV change is recorded in the P & L but requires the changes in the own credit risk to be included in the appendix. Consequently, the difference between AC and FVTPL using IAS 39 is the degree of changes transferred into the P & L which is booked against equity. Deposits from customers measured in line with IFRS 9 remain partly the same. Therefore, the approach for the measurement at AC is consistent with IAS 39. In contrast, the measurement at FVTPL using the FVO leads to the separation of FV changes attributable to the P & L and FV changes due to the own credit risk allocated into the OCI which is not intended to be recycled.

The second financial liability is deposits from banks which is similar to deposits from customers as it is also affected by the maturity transformation, liquidity and interest rate risk. The measurement at AC and FVTPL for IAS 39 and IFRS 9 indicate the same findings as for deposits from customers.

With respect to own issuances, the relevant influencing and impacting factors are the interest rate risk and the time until a bond matures. Generally, own issuances are recorded at FV including the transaction costs for the initial recognition if the financial liability becomes part of a contractual agreement. While the derecognition is consistent with deposits from customers, the repurchase of own issuances by the issuer is also considered as derecognition and the difference between the acquisition cost and book value of the issued bond is recorded in the P & L. The measurement is in line with IAS 39 either at AC or at FVTPL if the FVO is exercised. The approach remains as for deposits from customers as the effective interest rate method is applied and disagio/agio affects the P & L. In contrast, FVTPL includes all FV changes in the P & L and illustrates the part attributable to the own credit risk in the appendix. Moreover, IFRS 9 is applied as for deposits from customers or banks leading to the measurement at AC which affects the P & L or the measurement at FVTPL which is relevant for the P & L and OCI.

In regard to the empirical analysis of this paper, deposits from customers, deposits from banks and own issuances, also referred to as debt securities issued of RBI AG and Erste Group AG are analysed in terms of classification and measurement in line with the financial statements. Furthermore, the central question – what the impact of IFRS 9 regarding liabilities is – is answered.

Generally, IFRS 9 effective since 1 January 2018 affects less parts of the liability side whereas the asset side showed significantly more changes. Consequently, for financial liabilities, the recording of profit and loss regarding the FVO changed in comparison to IAS 39. While exceptions for the FV measurement of financial liabilities exist in regard to the subsequent measurement, the focus in this paper is the change from AC to FV. Thereby the focus is solely set on the FVO. With respect to the theoretical examination of deposits from customers, deposits from banks and own issuances, no considerable difference is illustrated in comparison to the empirical analysis in terms of classification and measurement.

Prior to the analysis, it is important to point that RBI AG applied IFRS 9.7.1.2 which prescribes the presentation of financial liabilities measured at FVTPL in 2017 whereas Erste Group AG did not conduct new standards prior to the date of effectiveness.

Regarding FV changes of financial liabilities designated at FVTPL due to changes in the own credit risk – attributable to the FVO chosen – RBI incurred a loss of EUR 0.14 million in 2017 which improved to EUR 0.03 million in 2018. In Q1 2019, RBI AG illustrated for FV changes due to changes in the own credit risk a gain of EUR 4 million. With respect to the assumption that the FVO and consequently the switch from AC to FV is applied, RBI AG instead decided to reclassify financial liabilities designated at FV, for which FV changes attributable to the own credit risk are booked into the OCI, to financial liabilities measured at AC. As a result, this reclassification lead to a significant improvement in the OCI for 2018.

For Erste Group AG, the FV changes are listed in the P & L which incurred a loss of EUR 22.6 million as a result from the measurement/repurchase of financial liabilities designated at FVTPL in 2017 whereas an improvement with a total of EUR 154.1 million is illustrated in 2018. The FV changes attributable to the own credit risk solely affect debt securities issued amounting to EUR 90.9 million in 2017 whereas no change is attributable to deposits from customers or banks. The FV changes attributable to the own credit risk changed in 2018 leading to a loss of EUR 1 million for deposits and a considerable drop to minus EUR 226 million for debt securities issued. Erste Group AG decided to present the FV changes due to the own credit risk within the OCI as own credit risk reserve which resulted in EUR 0.23 million due to cumulative amounts recorded but lead to a deterioration in Q1 2019 resulting in a loss of EUR 0.03 million.

The main findings in regard to IFRS 9 and the empirical analysis indicate that financial liabilities designated at FVTPL are reclassified into the measurement at AC within RBI AG whereas Erste Group AG decided to reclassify financial instruments at AC to financial instruments measured at FVTPL, thereby exercising the FVO which requires FV changes due to the own credit risk to be booked into the OCI. However, deposits from customers account for the highest proportion on the liability side and are in line with deposits from banks and debt securities issued for the most part measured at AC for both RBI AG and Erste Group AG.

Comparing the figures of Q1 2019 for RBI AG with a gain and Erste Group AG showing a loss, the decision to exercise the FVO and the result of Erste Group AG might be attributable to the credit risk or is due to the degree of financial liabilities reclassified at FVTPL. It is therefore reasonable to assume that RBI AG reclassified financial liabilities to the measurement at AC in order to illustrate changes in the P & L instead of the OCI which might contributed to a gain. Nevertheless, as described in the current state of research, the OCI might be considered as position for volatility which is used as substitute to the P & L and consequently requires the analysis of the OCI for a longer period. With respect to the methodical approach, the findings in the paper are based on a qualitive research chosen for the empirical analysis. Furthermore, the findings are restricted due to the small number of banks decided on and the geographical focus on Austrian banks. Another restriction is attributable to the number of financial statements analysed.

Bibliography

Anderson, Jenny, and Landon Thomas Jr. 2007. "Goldman Sachs Rakes in Profit in Credit Crisis." *The New York Times*, 2007. Accessed September 07, 2018. https://nyti.ms/2yBkiFZ.

Becker, Klaus, and Gero Wiechens. 2008. "Fair Value-Option Auf Eigene Verbindlichkeiten." *Zeitschrift für kapitalmarktorientierte Rechnungslegung* (10): 625–30. https://www.wiso-net.de/dosearch?dbShortcut=KOR&q=1617-8084.IS.+AND+2008.YR.+AND+10.HN.+AND+625.SE.&explicitSearch=true #KOR__080625A. Accessed August 29, 2018.

Bessis, Joël. 2010. *Risk Management in Banking.* 3. ed., reprinted. Chichester: Wiley.

Blecher, Christian. 2018. "The Influence of Uncertainty on the Standard-Setting Decision Between Fair Value and Historical Cost Accounting Under Asymmetric Information." *Rev Quant Finan Acc* 55 (Special Issue): 66. Accessed July 20, 2018. Accessed July 20, 2018. doi:10.1007/s11156-018-0742-5.

Bohn, Andreas, Marije Elkenbracht-Huizing, and Maria Adler, eds. 2014. *The Handbook of ALM in Banking: Interest Rates, Liquidity and the Balance Sheet.* London: Risk Books a Division of Incisive Media Investments.

Bohn, Andreas, and Paolo Tonucci. 2014. "ALM Within a Constrained Balance Sheet." In *the Handbook of ALM in Banking: Interest Rates, Liquidity and the Balance Sheet*, edited by Andreas Bohn, Marije Elkenbracht-Huizing, and Maria Adler, 59–82. London: Risk Books a Division of Incisive Media Investments.

Boissieu, Christian de. 2017. "The Banking Union Revisited." In Financial Regulation in the EU: From Resilience to Growth, edited by Raphaël Douady, Clément Goulet, and Pierre-Charles Pradier, 85–107. Cham: Springer International Publishing. Accessed July 20, 2018.

Bratten, Brian, Monika Causholli, and Urooj Khan. 2016. "Usefulness of Fair Values for Predicting Banks' Future Earnings: Evidence from Other Comprehensive Income and Its Components." *Rev Account Stud* 21 (1): 280–315. Accessed August 29, 2018. doi:10.1007/s11142-015-9346-7.

Choudhry, Moorad. 2007. *Bank Asset and Liability Management: Strategy, Trading, Analysis.* Hoboken: John Wiley & Sons.

Deloitte & Touche GmbH Wirtschaftsprüfungsgesellschaft. 2011. "IFRS 9 Finanzinstrumente: Ein Praxisleitfaden Für Finanzdienstleister." https://www.iasplus.com/de/publications/german-publications/other/ifrs-9-praxisleitfaden-fuer-finanzdienstleister/file. Accessed August 28, 2018.

Deloitte & Touche GmbH Wirtschaftsprüfungsgesellschaft. 2014. "IFRS Fokussiert: IFRS 9 – Neue Vorschriften Zur Bilanzierung Von Finanzinstrumenten." https://www.iasplus.com/de/publications/german-publications/ifrs-fokussiert/ifrs-9/at_download/file/IFRS_fokussiert_Nr_1_7_2014_safe.pdf. Accessed July 23, 2018.

Detzen, Dominic. 2016. "From Compromise to Concept? – a Review of 'Other Comprehensive Income'." *Accounting and Business Research* 46 (7): 760–83. Accessed August 29, 2018. doi:10.1080/00014788.2015.1135783.

Doralt, Werner, ed. 2018. *IAS/IFRS, Internationale Rechnungslegung 2018/19.* 21. Auflage, Stand 1.5.2018. Kodex des internationalen Rechts.

Douady, Raphaël, Clément Goulet, and Pierre-Charles Pradier, eds. 2017. *Financial Regulation in the EU: From Resilience to Growth.* Cham: Springer International Publishing. Accessed July 20, 2018. http://dx.doi.org/10.1007/978-3-319-44287-7.

Enthofer, Hannes, and Patrick Haas. 2016. *Asset Liability Management, Gesamtbanksteuerung: Handbuch = Asset Liability Management, Total Bank Management; Handbook.* Wien: Linde international.

Erste Group Bank AG. 2019a. "Annual Report 2018." Accessed June 06, 2019. https://www.erstegroup.com/content/dam/at/eh/www_erstegroup_com/en/Investor%20Relations/2018/Reports/AR2018_FINAL_en.pdf.

Erste Group Bank AG. 2019b. "Interim Report First Quarter 2019." Accessed June 06, 2019. https://www.erstegroup.com/content/dam/at/eh/www_erstegroup_com/en/Investor%20Relations/2019/Reports/IR_Interim_Report_EG_Q119en.pdf.

Erste Group Bank AG. 2018. "Annual Report 2017." Accessed June 06, 2019. https://www.erstegroup.com/content/dam/at/eh/www_erstegroup_com/en/Investor%20Relations/2017/Reports/AR2017_FINAL_en.pdf.

European Central Bank. 2019. "List of Supervised Entities: Cut-Off Date for Changes: 1 June 2019." Accessed July 10, 2019. https://www.bankingsupervision.europa.eu/ecb/pub/pdf/ssm.listofsupervisedentities20190601.en.pdf.

Farag, Marc, Damian Harland, and Dan Nixon. 2014. "Bank Capital and Liquidity." In *the Handbook of ALM in Banking: Interest Rates, Liquidity and the Balance Sheet*, edited by Andreas Bohn, Marije Elkenbracht-Huizing, and Maria Adler, 25–57. London: Risk Books a Division of Incisive Media Investments.

Gentili, Giovanni, and Nicola Santini. 2014. "Measuring and Managing Interest Rate and Basis Risk." In *the Handbook of ALM in Banking: Interest Rates, Liquidity and the Balance Sheet*, edited by Andreas Bohn, Marije Elkenbracht-Huizing, and Maria Adler, 85–121. London: Risk Books a Division of Incisive Media Investments.

Gruber, Bernhard, and Christian Engelbrechtsmüller, eds. 2016. *IFRS 9 Finanzinstrumente - Herausforderungen Für Banken.* With the assistance of E. Aschauer, D. Börstler, T. Gaber, C. I. Grinschgl, M. Hadeyer, P. Kudrna, W. Reitgruber et al. Wien: Linde.

Hartmann-Wendels, Thomas, Andreas Pfingsten, and Martin Weber. 2015. *Bankbetriebslehre.* 6. Auflage. Berlin, Heidelberg: Springer.

Heesen, Bernd. 2017. *Basiswissen Bilanzanalyse: Schneller Einstieg in Jahresabschluss, Bilanz Und GuV.* 2. Auflage. Wiesbaden: Springer Gabler. Accessed July 20, 2018. http://dx.doi.org/10.1007/978-3-658-17227-5.

Heidorn, Thomas, and Christian Schäffler. 2017. *Finanzmathematik in Der Bankpraxis: Vom Zins Zur Option.* 7. Auflage. Wiesbaden: Springer Gabler. Accessed July 18, 2018. http://dx.doi.org/10.1007/978-3-658-13448-8.

Horngren, Charles T., Gary L. Sundem, John A. Elliott, and Donna R. Philbrick. 2014. *Introduction to Financial Accounting.* 11. ed., Pearson new internat. ed. Pearson custom library. Harlow: Pearson.

Institut der Wirtschaftsprüfer. 2018. *International Financial Reporting Standards IFRS: Einschließlich International Accounting Standards IAS Und Interpretationen: Die Amtlichen EU-Texte Englisch-Deutsch.* 11., aktualisierte Auflage, Stand: 1. Dezember 2017. IDW Textausgabe.

International Accounting Standards Board. 2009. "IASB Completes First Phase of Financial Instruments Accounting Reform." News release. November 12, 2009. Accessed July 24, 2018. https://www.iasplus.com/en/binary/pressrel/0911ifrs9.pdf.

Kemp, Malcolm H.D. 2017. *Systemic Risk: A Practitioner's Guide to Measurement, Management and Analysis.* London: Palgrave Macmillan UK. Accessed July 18, 2018. http://dx.doi.org/10.1057/978-1-137-56587-7.

Kirsten, Björn. 2016. "Zum Bilanzpolitischen Potential Von Zinsinstrumenten in Der IFRS-Bankbilanz." In *Zum Bilanzpolitischen Potential Von Zinsinstrumenten in Der IFRS-Bankbilanz*, edited by Manfred J. Matschke, Thomas Hering, Michael Olbrich, Heinz E. Klingelhöfer, and Gerrit Brösel. Finanzwirtschaft, Unternehmensbewertung & Revisionswesen. Wiesbaden: Springer Fachmedien Wiesbaden. Dissertation. 10.1007/978-3-658-11675-0. Accessed July 17, 2018.

Kobialka, Marek. 2017. "FINREP Unter IFRS 9." In *Meldewesen Für Finanzinstitute: Was Bringt Die Neue Europäische Aufsicht?* edited by Christian Cech and Silvia Helmreich, 225–39. Wiesbaden: Springer Gabler. Accessed July 20, 2018.

Koulafetis, Panayiota. 2017. *Modern Credit Risk Management: Theory and Practice.* London: Palgrave Macmillan UK. Accessed July 17, 2018. https://link.springer.com/content/pdf/10.1057%2F978-1-137-52407-2.pdf.

Lane, Sarah, and Mark Kennedy. 2015. "IFRS 9: A SOLUTION to PAST SHORTCOMINGS?" *Accountancy Ireland* 47 (6): 30–32. https://search.proquest.com/docview/1755076385?rfr_id=info%3Axri%2Fsid%3Aprimo. Accessed August 29, 2018.

Massari, Mario, Gianfranco Gianfrate, and Laura Zanetti. 2014. *The Valuation of Financial Companies: Tools and Techniques to Measure the Value of Banks, Insurance Companies, and Other Financial Institutions.* Wiley finance series. Chichester: Wiley.

Matschke, Manfred J., Thomas Hering, Michael Olbrich, Heinz E. Klingelhöfer, and Gerrit Brösel, eds. 2016. *Zum Bilanzpolitischen Potential Von Zinsinstrumenten in Der IFRS-Bankbilanz.* Finanzwirtschaft, Unternehmensbewertung & Revisionswesen. Wiesbaden: Springer Fachmedien Wiesbaden. Dissertation. Accessed July 17, 2018. http://dx.doi.org/10.1007/978-3-658-11675-0.

Matthews, Kent, and John L. Thompson. 2008. *The Economics of Banking*. 2. ed., [rev. and updated]. Chichester: Wiley.

Mishkin, Frederic S. 2016. *The Economics of Money, Banking, and Financial Markets*. Eleventh edition, Global edition. Boston: Pearson.

Mobius, Mark. 2012. *Bonds: An Introduction to the Core Concepts*. Mark Mobius masterclass. Singapore: John Wiley & Sons Singapore.

Mondello, Enzo. 2017. *Finance: Theorie Und Anwendungsbeispiele*. Lehrbuch. Wiesbaden: Springer Gabler. Accessed July 17, 2018. http://dx.doi.org/10.1007/978-3-658-13199-9.

Müller, Stefan, and Patrick Saile. 2018. *Internationale Rechnungslegung (IFRS)*. Studienwissen kompakt. Wiesbaden: Springer Gabler. Accessed July 20, 2018. http://dx.doi.org/10.1007/978-3-658-17361-6.

Oesterreichische Nationalbank. 2018. "Fakten Zu Österreich Und Seinen Banken: Oktober 2017 – Kennzahlen-Update Jänner 2018." Accessed July 10, 2019. https://www.oenb.at/dam/jcr:2c3a1a2b-8fd1-4e3b-a0c9-ddce77182c32/fakten_zu_oesterreich_und_seinen_banken_april_2019.pdf.

Población García, Francisco J. 2017. *Financial Risk Management: Identification, Measurement and Management*. Cham: Springer International Publishing. Accessed July 17, 2018. https://link.springer.com/content/pdf/10.1007%2F978-3-319-41366-2.pdf.

PricewaterhouseCoopers Aktiengesellschaft Wirtschaftsprüfungsgesellschaft. 2017a. *IFRS Für Banken - Band I: Praxishandbuch Der Bankbilanzierung Nach IFRS*. 6. Auflage. Köln, Frankfurt am Main: Bank-Verlag GmbH; pwc PricewaterhouseCoopers GmbH Wirtschaftsprüfungsgesellschaft.

PricewaterhouseCoopers Aktiengesellschaft Wirtschaftsprüfungsgesellschaft. 2017b. *IFRS Für Banken - Band II: Praxishandbuch Der Bankbilanzierung Nach IFRS*. 6. Auflage. Köln, Frankfurt am Main: Bank-Verlag GmbH; pwc PricewaterhouseCoopers GmbH Wirtschaftsprüfungsgesellschaft.

Raiffeisen Bank International AG. 2019a. "Annual Report 2018." Accessed June 10, 2019. http://investor.rbinternational.com/fileadmin/ir/2018_FY/2019-03-13_2018_Annual_Report_RBI.pdf.

Raiffeisen Bank International AG. 2019b. "First Quarter Report 2019." Accessed June 10, 2019. http://investor.rbinternational.com/fileadmin/ir/2019_Q1/2019-05-15_Q1_Report_RBI.pdf.

Raiffeisen Bank International AG. 2018. "Annual Report 2017." Accessed June 10, 2019. http://investor.rbinternational.com/fileadmin/ir/2017_FY/2018-03-14_2017_Annual_Report_RBI.pdf.

Rose, Peter S., and Sylvia C. Hudgins. 2013. *Bank Management & Financial Services*. 9. ed., internat. ed. New York, NY: McGraw-Hill.

Sagerschnig, Martin. 2016. "Grundlagen Zur Bilanzierung Von Finanzinstrumenten Nach IFRS." In *IFRS 9 Finanzinstrumente - Herausforderungen Für Banken*, edited by Bernhard Gruber and Christian Engelbrechtsmüller, 1–29. Wien: Linde.

Schneider, Felix, and Duc H. Tran. 2015. "On the Relation Between the Fair Value Option and Bid-Ask Spreads: Descriptive Evidence on the Recognition of Credit Risk Changes Under IFRS." *J Bus Econ* 85 (9): 1049–81. Accessed August 29, 2018. doi:10.1007/s11573-015-0776-2.

Tian, Weidong, ed. 2017. *Commercial Banking Risk Management: Regulation in the Wake of the Financial Crisis.* New York, s.l. Palgrave Macmillan US. Accessed July 20, 2018. http://dx.doi.org/10.1057/978-1-137-59442-6.

Wagenhofer, Alfred. 2018. "IAS/IFRS, Internationale Rechnungslegung 2018/19." In *IAS/IFRS, Internationale Rechnungslegung 2018/19*, edited by Werner Doralt. 21. Auflage, Stand 1.5.2018. Kodex des internationalen Rechts.

Whitedec, Ben. 2008. "Goldman Sachs Reports $2.1 Billion Quarterly Loss." *The New York Times*. https://nyti.ms/2MYLV7q. Accessed September 07, 2018.

Wu, Wei, Nicole Thibodeau, and Robert Couch. 2016. "An Option for Lemons? The Fair Value Option for Liabilities During the Financial Crisis." *Journal of Accounting, Auditing & Finance* 31 (4): 441–82. Accessed August 29, 2018. doi:10.1177/0148558X16645994.

Zülch, Henning, and Matthias Hendler. 2017. *Bilanzierung Nach International Financial Reporting Standards (IFRS).* 2. Auflage. Weinheim, Germany: Wiley-VCH Verlag GmbH

Table of figures

List of tables

List of equations